# ZAMBEZI
## RIVER OF AFRICA

# ZAMBEZI
## RIVER OF AFRICA

Mike Coppinger and Jumbo Williams

NEW
HOLLAND

 This edition published in 1994 by
New Holland (Publishers) Ltd
London • Cape Town • Sydney

ISBN 1 85368 296 9

New Holland (Publishers) Ltd
37 Connaught Street, London W2 2AZ

Editor: Jan Schaafsma
Designer: Neville Poulter
Typesetting by Theiner Typesetting (Pty) Ltd, Tygerpark
Reproduction supervised by Tien Wah Press (Pte) Ltd, Singapore
Printed and bound in Singapore by Tien Wah Press (Pte) Ltd

4

HALF TITLE PAGE *Whitefronted Bee-eaters are gregarious birds that burrow their
nests into sand cliffs. Suitable breeding sites are utilized at numerous points along
the Zambezi.*

TITLE PAGE *The natural reservoir of the Zambezi floodplain in western Zambia
plays an important role in regulating the river's flow. It also nurtures abundant fish
and bird populations and sustains the local fishing and cattle-rearing inhabitants.*

ABOVE *Although it has had a negative ecological impact in some respects, man-made
Lake Kariba has many positive aspects as well, supporting thriving wildlife communities, for example. The fishing and tourism industries have capitalized on nature's
bounty.*

RIGHT *An over-ambitious attempt to ford a floodplain channel brought 'Whimbrel'
to a spluttering halt. Mike searches hopefully for a solution, while intrigued villagers
flock to the unusual spectacle.*

*Ever since God created the world, his invisible qualities, both*
*his eternal power and his divine nature, have been clearly seen;*
*they are perceived in the things that God has made.*
Romans 1:20

## ACKNOWLEDGEMENTS

One of the immeasurable benefits of adventure travel is the opportunities one is afforded to befriend individuals from many different walks of life and exchange ideas with them. Our expedition spanned half a decade and it is a source of regret that it is impossible for us to list all those who offered us companionship and spiritual or material assistance during that time. To these people we sincerely say a collective thank you – without your support our endeavours would have floundered hopelessly.

We received a generous private donation from the late A.I. Hepburn, while companies that assisted us were Young Yamaha, Imperial Motors, Comcon and Photoworld, all of Durban. Multivisio (Durban) helped us immensely with our photographic work. The Zimbabwe Ornithological Society awarded us a grant and the Endangered Wildlife Trust provided funds for us to conduct aerial counts of dolphin and dugong on the delta.

We often operated within protected areas and access to many regions would have been impossible without the permission and assistance of government authorities. We therefore gratefully thank the Zimbabwe Department of National Parks and Wildlife Management, the Zambian National Parks and Wildlife Service, the Department of Agriculture and Nature Conservation of Namibia, and the Mozambique Directorate of Forestry and Wildlife.

While in Caprivi, we enjoyed the splendid hospitality of the South African Defence Force and our gratitude is especially extended to Captain Andre White who not only piloted our Wattled Crane census but also became a true friend, Jackie Wright who organised our trip on the naval barge to Mpalela, and conservationist Neil Macdonald who led us safely into the depths of the Linyanti swamps, where he almost single-handedly tackled a great many armed poachers.

Paul Connelly of Shearwater, Zimbabwe, first introduced us to grade V white-water action, and the Anglo American Company and Sobek (both of Zambia) sponsored our rafting trip in the gorges below Victoria Falls.

From the conception of the expedition Professor Gordon Maclean sustained us with his positive advice and superb ornithological skills, and we also received expert assistance from the following: Dylan Aspinwall, Fay and Kevin Dunham, John Hargrove, Geoff Howard, Kit Hustler, Brian Marshall, John Mendelsohn, John Orpen, Dave Rockingham-Gill, Michael Stuart Irwin, Russell Taylor and Ken Tinley. Furthermore the staff of the Zimbabwe National Parks Library were most helpful.

Many kind folk made available their homes, safari camps, tents, vehicles, planes and boats, and we are most grateful to them. If we do not mention you by name, please don't think that you are forgotten! At the Zambezi's source, the hospitality and generosity of the Fisher family remains a legend, and other missionaries, too, gave us succour during our time on the Upper Zambezi, particularly at Chavuma, Chinyingi, Zambezi Boma, Lukulu, Mongu and Sioma. Grace and Dave Croudace have a very special place in our hearts.

In Zambia we repeatedly imposed ourselves on several long-suffering friends. These include Trish and Paul Harrison, Carol and John Coppinger, Pam and John Adams. Likewise, in Zimbabwe we are deeply indebted to Julie and Dave Glynn, Pam and Chris Lewis, Francois Flanagan, Mrs and Dr MacGibbon (Sr), Sharon and Dave Olsen, Fay and Kevin Dunham, Lynne and Russell Taylor, and Aiden Hogg. We stayed virtually free at several safari camps, and wish to thank the Mashonaland Hunting Association as well as the Rukomechi, Spurwing, Western and Mozambique Safaris. Steve Edwards accompanied us on Cahora Bassa, before his epic Messenguezi-Kafukudzi walk; Craig Saunders proved wild men do make the best pilots; and at the delta in Mozambique we were fortunate enough to be with Sansao Bonito – without his willing assistance we would hardly have accomplished anything at all, for our knowledge of Portuguese is abysmal. Stewart Hogan kindly accommodated us in Beira when we were stranded without aviation fuel, and Ken Tinley helped Mike enormously in Maputo, providing not only lodging, but also nightly recitals on his didgeridoo!

There are several people close to us who gave unstintingly of their time and support. We thank Jane and Bill Clegg, Brigid and Pete Turner, Wendy and Paula Miles, and Joanne Coppinger with all our heart. We thank our parents for providing the background which equipped us for this undertaking and for their support throughout the project.

Finally, thanks to Struik Publishers, with whom it has been a pleasure to work; they have made every effort to truthfully represent the elusive essence of the Rio Zambeze. The completion of this work was great fun and represents the culmination of our expedition - we hope the book similarly brings you both enjoyment and an appreciation of the great Zambezi.

MIKE COPPINGER AND JUMBO WILLIAMS   DURBAN, MAY 1991

*'... scenes so lovely must have been gazed on by angels in their flight.'* David Livingstone.

# CONTENTS

LEFT *Highlands straddling the Zaïre-Zambia border form a watershed between the Zambezi and Zaïre rivers. Numerous energetic streams tumble down the hills, joining forces and rapidly building the stature of the two giants.*

# INTRODUCTION

*Mike Coppinger*

ELEPHANT TRACKS WERE STAMPED deeply into the coarse beach sand. Jumbo tied our boat to a drowned tree at the water's edge, then we climbed barefoot onto the boulders rimming the cove. Lake Cahora Bassa, alluring and virtually unexplored, unfolded eastwards and beckoned us to venture further into her vastness. We made up our minds – this would be our next camp site.

After unloading our fuel drums we manoeuvred the boat through the submerged tree line, then turned west towards our current base. A slight breeze was not sufficient to disturb the water and our craft skimmed easily across the surface. We kept a wary distance from the north bank – that was bandit country. Renamo rebels roamed there freely, which was why we were alone on the lake.

The evening light transformed the lake into a sheet of rippled gold, broken sporadically by clouds of spray puffed into the air by wallowing hippo. Overhead, egrets heading for their roosts shone white against a turquoise sky. From the shoreline emanated the gentle whistle of Whitefaced Duck.

Jumbo broke our silence, 'This sort of thing makes it all worthwhile.'

That summed it up: the privilege of being surrounded by the splendid perfection of nature, the excitement of exploring little-known lands and waters, tinged with the thrill of surviving the threats of dangerous men and animals. The hardships were worth it.

LEFT *Stark basalt walls in the Batoka Gorge compress the Zambezi into a surging torrent, in some places only 10 metres wide. Wild rapids make for breathtaking rafting as the river descends 350 metres between Victoria Falls and Kariba.*
ABOVE *Our rubber dinghy was well suited to the expedition's requirements.*

I had traversed the Zambezi valley many times in my younger days as I travelled between home in Lusaka and school in Salisbury (Harare). Jumbo had a more intimate knowledge of the river, born of school expeditions and social outings on the Zimbabwean portion of the water-way. To both of us it had always been a symbol of dramatic, untarnished wilderness. However, by 1984 our ties with central Africa had become tenuous. Jumbo's career as an anaesthetist, and mine as a computer consultant, had led us both south of the tropics to Durban.

I think many city dwellers occasionally feel an urge to 'get away from it all' – to 'go natural'. Our motivation was more than that. At the age of 33 we perceived that aspects of life we held dear, things that we really enjoyed, were being sidelined. Circumstances were steering us into neglect of our interest in nature as the tentacles of professional success and a somewhat sterile 'security' began to creep over our lives. It suddenly became clear that we had to do something positive and definite to realize our dreams, or allow them to be insidiously washed away by the tide of expediency.

We sought a natural experience. We wanted to live outdoors – to feel the changes in the wind, use the sun and moon as our chronometers, allow tropical rain to splash against our skin, feel the adrenalin course through our veins when encountering wild animals on their terms. Beyond that, we yearned to fill some of the gaps in our understanding of the ecological dynamics of nature. We wished to develop a more holistic comprehension of life, the planet and the subcontinent.

The decision was made – we would call the urban bluff, step off the treadmill and dedicate two years to the study of nature 'somewhere in Africa'. We required a theme for our activities and felt a desire to apply

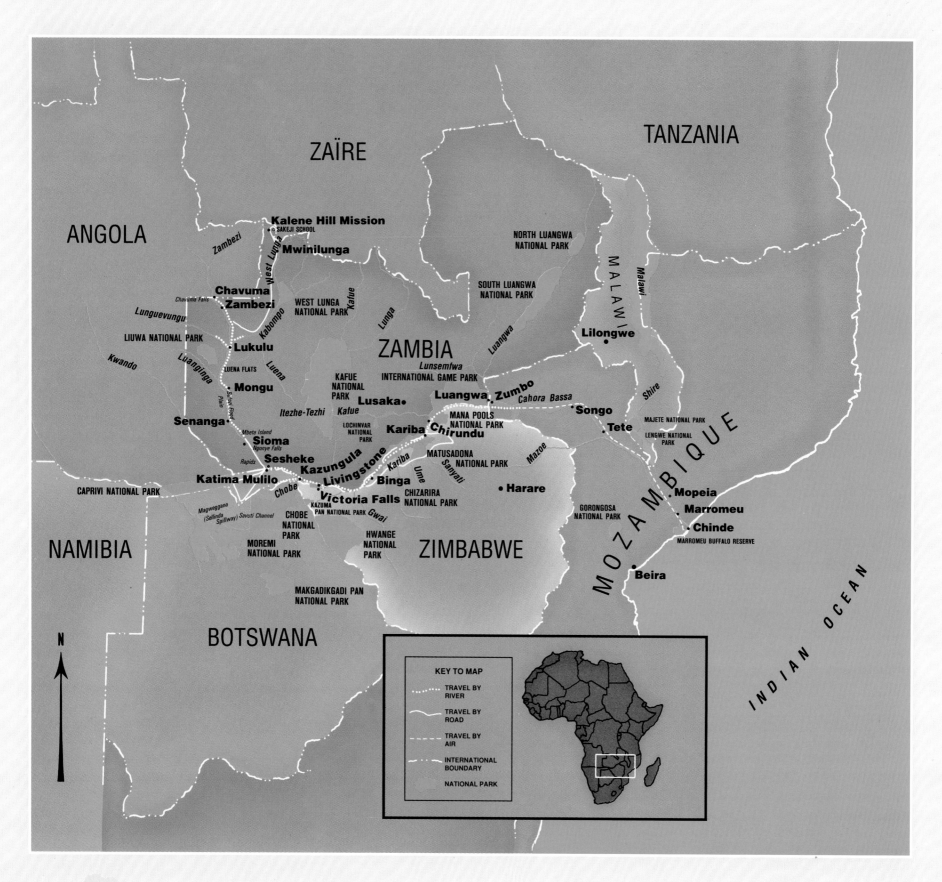

ANGOLA

ZAÏRE

TANZANIA

Kalene Hill Mission
SAKEJI SCHOOL
Zambezi
West Lunga
Mwinilunga

NORTH LUANGWA
NATIONAL PARK

Chavuma
Chavuma Falls
Zambezi
Lunguevungu
Kabompo
WEST LUNGA
NATIONAL PARK
Kafue

SOUTH LUANGWA
NATIONAL PARK

MALAWI
Malawi

LIUWA NATIONAL PARK
Lukulu
Luena FLATS
Luena
Luena

Lunga

ZAMBIA

Luangwa

Lilongwe

Kwando
Luanginga
Mongu

Lunsemfwa
INTERNATIONAL GAME PARK

KAFUE
NATIONAL
PARK

Shire

Bulozi Flood
Plain

Itezhe-Tezhi

Kafue

Lusaka

Luangwa

Zumbo
Cahora Bassa

Songo

Senanga
Mbeta Island

LOCHINVAR
NATIONAL
PARK

MANA POOLS
NATIONAL PARK

Tete

MAJETE NATIONAL PARK

Sioma
Ngonye Falls

Kariba
Chirundu

LENGWE NATIONAL
PARK

M
O
Z
A
M
B
I
Q
U
E

Rapids
Sesheke

Kariba

Ume

MATUSADONA
NATIONAL PARK

Mazoe

Katima Mulilo
Kazungula
Livingstone

Chobe

Sanyati

CAPRIVI NATIONAL PARK

Binga

Harare

Mopeia

Victoria Falls
KAZUMA
PAN NATIONAL PARK

CHIZARIRA
NATIONAL PARK

Gwai

GORONGOSA
NATIONAL PARK

Marromeu

Magweggana
(Sellinda
Spillway) Savuti Channel

CHOBE
NATIONAL
PARK

Chinde

NAMIBIA

MOREMI
NATIONAL PARK

HWANGE
NATIONAL
PARK

ZIMBABWE

MARROMEU BUFFALO RESERVE

Beira

MAKGADIKGADI PAN
NATIONAL PARK

I
N
D
I
A
N
O
C
E
A
N

BOTSWANA

N

KEY TO MAP

- - - - - TRAVEL BY
RIVER

TRAVEL BY
ROAD

- - - - - TRAVEL BY
AIR

- · - · - INTERNATIONAL
BOUNDARY

NATIONAL PARK

ourselves to constructive endeavour. It was a short step to selecting the Zambezi as our subject. We feared that the character of the mighty river was changing fast and that the opportunity to savour its pristine qualities was rapidly fading.

The full 2 700-kilometre length of the waterway had never been comprehensively explored owing to difficulty of access. Obstacles posed by harsh terrain, tumultuous waters, disease and wild animals have often been compounded by political problems. Zimbabwe's attainment of independence in 1980 eased the security situation to such a degree that we felt could just make a source-to-mouth journey feasible. We would certainly give it a try.

Arising in the north-western corner of Zambia, the Zambezi pushes westwards at first before being channeled south and then swinging east-wards across the continent to become the largest African river debouch-ing into the Indian Ocean. It washes the soil of six countries – Zambia, Angola, Namibia, Botswana, Zimbabwe and Mozambique – and also derives drainage from Malawi and Tanzania via the Shire tributary.

The flow carries water from the relatively wet areas of central Africa to the drier regions of the south. As one moves downstream away from the equator and to lower ground, the rainfall gradient declines. This is amply illustrated by the mean annual rainfall of 1 480 millimetres at the source, 1 400 millimetres at Chavuma, 716 millimetres at Victoria Falls, 600-700 millimetres in the Middle Zambezi and 610 millimetres at Tete. The coastal influence, however, increases precipitation at Chinde to 1 099 millimetres.

The Zambezi is the fourth largest river system in Africa, after the Nile, Zaïre and Niger. Its unique value lies in the fact that it is less developed than the others in terms of human settlement, and that ex-tensive areas along its banks enjoy protected status.

The length of the river can for convenience be divided into three sec-tions. The upper river extends from the source to the Victoria Falls. The young stream tumbles more than 270 metres in altitude on the first 100 kilometres of its journey. The course flattens out along its 300-kilometre passage through Angola, where it accumulates the bulk of its headwater drainage. Geologically, the Upper Zambezi passes through a major basin of sedimentation which also extends over much of Angola and northern Botswana. The basin is overspread by deposits of the Kalahari system, predominantly sands and sandstones. Two major features of this part of the river are the Zambezi floodplain and the Caprivi swamps. These vast wetlands play an important role in regulating the flow between dry and wet seasons, but also cause great water loss through evaporation.

The upper river has been spared major development and for the most part is remarkably free of pollution. However, wildlife upstream of the Chobe confluence is sparse and the banks are thinly populated by subsis-tence agriculturists and fishermen.

Many of the 84 fish species found in the Upper Zambezi also occur in the Okavango and Kafue basins which fall into the same zoogeographic area in terms of fish distribution. This grouping shows close similarities with the fish found within the southern tributaries of the Zaïre river. In the Middle Zambezi there are 69 species (45 of which are shared with the upper section) and these are more closely allied with the fish found in the lower river.

The middle zone supports one of Africa's most important wilderness areas. It consists essentially of a number of gorges, Lake Kariba and a wide, flat river section below the dam. Extensive areas of protected land on the Zimbabwean bank constitute sanctuaries harbouring the river's most prolific wildlife. Added to this is a recently proclaimed national park on the Zambian side in the lower reaches of the section.

Zimbabwe in particular has made good use of the wilderness resources to generate much needed revenue from adventure travel, photographic safaris and hunting. Lake Kariba has also been developed into an impor-tant commercial fishery.

Although the soils of the Middle Zambezi floodplain are relatively fer-tile, the harsh environment and low rainfall mitigate against commercial agriculture. For example, a sugar growing scheme established at Chi-rundu in the 1960s failed because of eelworm infestation and its remote-ness from viable markets.

Lake Cahora Bassa, sometimes placed within the middle section, is treated for the purposes of this book as constituting the upstream limit of the Lower Zambezi. The gorge in which the dam wall stands marks the river's descent from the central African plateau and from its base the gra-dient to the sea is gradual. Along this section there is more human settle-ment than is the case upstream, and a number of towns line the river, the largest being Tete and Marromeu.

Wildlife is limited, the most notable concentration occurring in the delta grasslands, where the remnants of vast herds of plains game still roam. We found that a relatively sparse animal population inhabits the shores of Lake Cahora Bassa.

For the past two decades the lower river has been racked by war. As a result the resources of Cahora Bassa have not yet been effectively uti-lized and the huge sugar industry that was developed around Marromeu has been seriously hamstrung.

The European world's first superficial encounter with Cuama, as the Portuguese originally knew the lower river, was when the seafarer Vasco da Gama reached Quelimane in 1498. In 1531 the Portuguese estab-lished a presence in the Arab settlement of Sena and in 1553 began to build at Tete. By the end of the sixteenth century the Portuguese con-tingent in each of these outposts numbered about 50. The river was a highway to the land of Monomatapa and carried traffic of gold, ivory and slaves.

João dos Santos, a Dominican friar who knew the territory well, visit-ed Tete around 1700. He recorded that the Kebrabassa rapids were not

13

LEFT *Dense reedbeds lining the lush river banks at the confluence of the Zambezi and Kabompo rivers provide good shelter for bream and other fish. Fishermen exploit the situation by placing their nets close to the water's edge.*
ABOVE *A feature of the Middle Zambezi are the hippos that sunbathe on sand-banks and islands and sometimes crash unexpectedly into the water when disturbed by passing boats.*

passable. He also noted that above the falls lay the region of Chicoa, reputed to be rich in silver, beyond which the river is again navigable – but nobody knew to where.

A better-known traveller, whose name has become irrevocably linked with the Zambezi, would have done well to peruse Santos' manuscripts. Dr David Livingstone's first encounter with the river was in 1851 when he reached Sesheke from South Africa. His travels took him upstream to the vicinity of the Lunguevungu from where he veered west to the

Angolan coast. From Luanda he doubled back and followed the flow right across the continent to the eastern seaboard, deviating from the river below Victoria Falls and again in the broken country surrounding Kebrabassa. These travels nurtured the missionary's dream to open up the river as 'God's Highway', via which Christianity could be brought to the people of the Dark Continent. Livingstone's second expedition, launched in 1858, accordingly employed a large flat-bottomed metal boat on which his party steamed upstream from the coast, but their dreams were shattered by the unnavigable gorge noted by Santos.

Another notable journey up the river, with few deviations, was made shortly afterwards by Major A. St. H. Gibbons. The party of 500 with which he started his expedition dwindled to four porters and five donkeys by the time he reached the source.

To achieve our objectives of detailed exploration, photography and scientific study, it was apparent that both land and water transport would be required. We also needed camping kit, photographic equipment and consumables plus sufficient funds to sustain ourselves on our travels. Financial assistance was clearly important, so we set about marketing our project to business enterprises.

Our salesmanship got virtually no response! We were, however, grateful for discount prices offered to us by certain dealers. Our approaches to conservation organizations for support received a cool reception - they were not prepared to align themselves with amateurs. But amongst the disappointment there was a shining example of remarkable generosity: an individual who had never met us, the late Mr A.I.M. Hepburn, made a donation of R4 000 to our cause.

We mustered our savings and invested in a rusty 1975 Land Cruiser, christened 'Whimbrel', a trailer named 'Pratincole', and a brand new Avon inflatable dinghy with a 25-horsepower Yamaha motor, appropriately named 'Skimmer'. The names betray our ornithological bias.

We both have a particular interest in birds and with the enthusiastic encouragement of Professor Gordon Maclean we compiled a research proposal. Our interest in avifauna proved to be a key to the endless fascination provided by our travels. We were to find that all areas offer some interesting facet of feathered life that warrants scrutiny. Furthermore, as our familiarity with bird species and their habitat preferences grew, so our perception of landscape variation was sharpened. Thus our predilection for bird life led us to an appreciation of the environment as a whole.

To the astonishment of friends who had witnessed our long drawn-out preparations, and endured repeated farewell parties, the two-man Zambezi River Expedition finally headed north from Durban in May 1986. Our rough itinerary was dictated by climatic and logistical considerations, which prohibited a sequential passage down the river. We had to grasp opportunities to access different areas as and when they arose.

We were to discover that roaming the African bush is not as straightforward as it might seem. Most wilderness areas are jealously guarded by either protective patrons or mind-numbing bureaucracy. In order to make possible the bushwhacking, considerable time and effort had to be expended on administrative and public relations activities.

Our wanderings in the first year took us from Katima Mulilo downstream to the Victoria Falls and thence from Kariba Gorge down to the Luangwa confluence. 'Whimbrel' conveyed us faithfully to strategic points on the river, where we would establish our tented camp. Generally we maintained a base for about two weeks, while we surveyed the river up and down in 'Skimmer' and explored the adjacent bushveld on foot. Sometimes our sorties on the boat extended over several days, in which case living conditions became more spartan as we slept under the stars and survived on basic rations.

We employed a three-legged iron pot as the primary instrument with which to inflict our culinary efforts upon each other. Fresh food was often not readily available, which compelled us to resort to dehydrated and tinned supplies. Jumbo's fabled expertise with the fishing rod did on occasion add appropriate variety to our diet.

By the end of the year our data collection included numbers and species of birds seen plus detailed notes of habitat types and human activity along the river banks. We had also begun specific studies of the breeding biology of two birds, the Rock Pratincole and African Skimmer, which were to remain subjects of special interest for us. The breeding of both these species is confined to the larger African rivers. They had never been comprehensively studied and in view of the threat posed to their breeding areas by planned dam construction we felt they warranted particular attention.

Shortly after the first thunderstorms of the season rumbled across the valley in late November we returned to Durban to spend the wet season

Phragmites mauritianus *characterizes much of the Zambezi shoreline.*

17

consolidating the material we had gathered, tending to our equipment and trying to generate funds from our photographs.

Four months later we were back in central Africa. Penetrating some of the most isolated parts of the continent we followed the river passage from its source down through western Zambia. Thereafter, journeys through the imposing gorges below Victoria Falls and the contrasting vastness of Lake Kariba completed our study of the Zambian and Zimbabwean portions of the river.

The Angolan civil war compelled us to skirt that country. As we detoured around it we compensated with a visit to the little-known West Lunga National Park. We were the first visitors in many years to reach the interior of the park, having hacked our own road. Evidence of poaching was widespread, particularly depressing being the fresh carcass of an elephant shot with an automatic weapon. Shortly after that distressing discovery we were apprehended at the local police chief's instruction, although our movements had been cleared with National Parks beforehand. We were nevertheless removed from the area and interrogated, before eventually being released.

Another incident which increased our wariness of officials occurred later in Lusaka. A gunshot at our door woke us at dawn one morning. With the sleep still in our eyes we were marched out of the house in our bedclothes and driven to C.I.D. headquarters at gunpoint. A very random interrogation followed after which we were released with the unlikely explanation that because we were strangers the police had wanted to get to know us better so that we could become friends!

Our visit to West Lunga National Park, which lies in the fork of the Kabompo and West Lunga rivers, was one of a number of deviations from the mainstream which gave us some familiarity with the Zambezi's major tributaries.

An excursion to the Shire River in Malawi took us from Zimbabwe through Mozambique's Tete corridor. Traffic traversing this war-torn area did so in armed convoy. Every week day a column of vehicles departed from the border post at either end of the corridor to converge on Tete. A bottleneck occurred while the heavy lorries from each direction crossed the Zambezi bridge one at a time. When we travelled north we waited four hours for the convoy of 150 vehicles to regroup. Then followed a nightmare dash from Tete to the Malawian border during which we were dwarfed and intimidated by massive trucks thundering out of the dust and passing us on either left or right as we tried to pick our way between landmine-blasted potholes. The threat posed by Re-

LEFT *The downstream limit of the Upper Zambezi is marked by a dramatic cascade over a basalt cliff 100 metres high. Livingstone Island offers an unusual view of the Victoria Falls when the water level is low.*
RIGHT *During the dry winter months extensive sandy beaches form on inside bends of the Upper Zambezi.*

namo ambushes paled into insignificance compared to the danger and damage caused by the drivers on the convoy.

Much safer were trips to the photographic safari camp managed by John and Carol, my brother and sister-in-law, on the Luangwa River. The muddy brown waters of the Luangwa course through eastern Zambia and its valley supports a wildlife population of remarkable diversity and abundance.

Another Zambian tributary rich with the blessings of nature is the Kafue. On visits to various points on the river we were always impressed by its unique character and the copious life it nurtures. At Lochinvar National Park on the Kafue Flats we were thrilled by the spectacle of several thousand lechwe grazing on the floodplain, and a bewildering array of waterbirds.

By early 1988 our funds were exhausted and we did not have the means to extend our travels to Mozambique. There was no option but to go back to earning an honest living. 'Whimbrel' made it to within 300 kilometres of Durban before collapsing in protest at two years of rugged hard labour. Three days of mechanical wizardry were needed to coax the vehicle into completing the final lap. Then, as we finally arrived home, the engine burst into flames!

Nearly three years later, in September 1990, the team reassembled. Jumbo had spent the intervening period furthering his medical career in the United States and my most notable achievement back in Durban had been marrying my wife, Joanne. 'Whimbrel's' body had been laid to rest, but her engine had been reconditioned and transferred to a cousin of identical vintage called 'Godwit'. We were ready for Mozambique.

Three months were all we could devote to the Lower Zambezi. Operating under volatile and unpredictable circumstances in a war-ravaged country, it was more difficult than ever to follow a predefined plan. However, in the final analysis we thankfully succeeded in achieving our key objectives.

By the time we witnessed the Zambezi's meeting with the Indian Ocean, seven years had elapsed since our commitment to the expedition had been made. Ultimately we had not achieved our goal of travelling the entire length of the great river. The 300 kilometres in Angola remained a mystery and nearly 700 kilometres of the Mozambican course had been seen only from the air.

Nonetheless, did we satisfy our underlying ambitions? We had certainly increased our understanding of the ecological web of nature, although from our new vantage point we could also see a lot more gaps in our knowledge. Lessons in fortitude and tolerance had increased our self-understanding and adjusted our priorities.

One of the joys of travel is the variety of people one encounters. We had the pleasure of meeting many fascinating characters, forming new friendships and renewing old ones. Some were very spiritual people whose influence, reinforced by our affinity with nature, brought us a great deal closer to God.

Yes, indeed – it was certainly worthwhile!

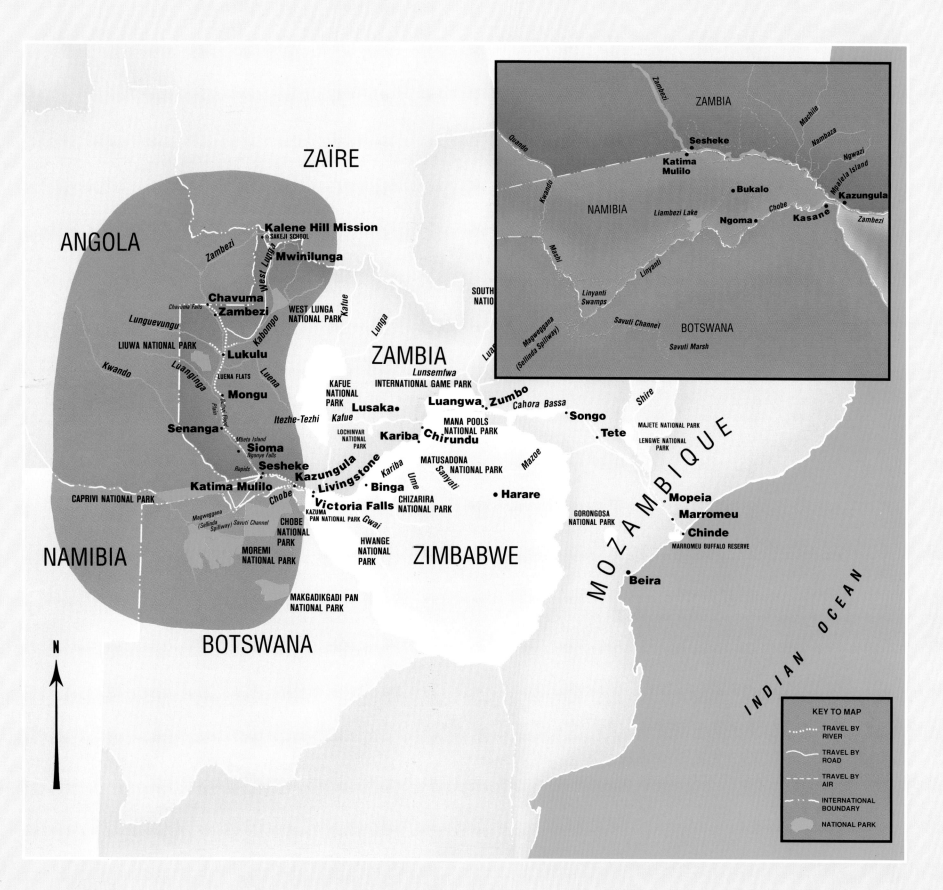

ZAÏRE

ANGOLA

Kalene Hill Mission
• SAKEJI SCHOOL
Mwinilunga
*Zambezi*
West Lunga
Chavuma
*Chavuma Falls*
Zambezi
WEST LUNGA
NATIONAL PARK
*Kafue*
*Kabompo*
*Lunguevungu*
*Lunga*
LIUWA NATIONAL PARK
ZAMBIA
*Luena*
Lukulu
*Luena Flats*
*Luanginga*
*Luena*
*Lunsemfwa*
INTERNATIONAL GAME PARK
KAFUE
NATIONAL
PARK
*Kwando*
Mongu
*Barotse Plain*
Senanga
*Itezhe-Tezhi*
*Kafue*
Lusaka
Luangwa• Zumbo
*Cahora Bassa*
Songo
Tete
*Shire*
MANA POOLS
NATIONAL PARK
MAJETE NATIONAL PARK
*Mbeta Island*
Sioma
*Ngonye Falls*
LOCHINVAR
NATIONAL
PARK
Karibar •Chirundu
LENGWE NATIONAL
PARK
*Rapids*
Sesheke
Kazungula
*Kariba*
MATUSADONA
NATIONAL PARK
*Mazoe*
Katima Mulilo
Livingstone
*Chobe*
Binga
*Ume*
*Sanyati*
•Harare
CAPRIVI NATIONAL PARK
Victoria Falls
*Magweggana (Sellinda Spillway)*
*Savuti Channel*
CHIZARIRA
NATIONAL PARK
KAZUMA
PAN NATIONAL PARK
*Gwai*
GORONGOSA
NATIONAL PARK
Mopeia
Marromeu
Chinde
MOZAMBIQUE
NAMIBIA
CHOBE
NATIONAL
PARK
HWANGE
NATIONAL
PARK
ZIMBABWE
MARROMEU BUFFALO RESERVE
MOREMI
NATIONAL
PARK
Beira
MAKGADIKGADI PAN
NATIONAL PARK
BOTSWANA
INDIAN OCEAN

N

SOUTH
NATIO...

Inset map:
*Zambezi*
ZAMBIA
*Machile*
*Quando*
Sesheke
*Nambaza*
Katima
Mulilo
*Ngwazi*
*Kwando*
•Bukalo
Mbalela Island
NAMIBIA
*Liambezi Lake*
*Chobe*
Kazungula
•Ngoma
Kasane
*Zambezi*
*Mashi*
*Linyanti*
*Magweggana (Sellinda Spillway)*
*Linyanti Swamps*
*Savuti Channel*
BOTSWANA
*Savuti Marsh*

KEY TO MAP
∙∙∙∙∙ TRAVEL BY RIVER
—— TRAVEL BY ROAD
- - - TRAVEL BY AIR
-∙∙-∙∙- INTERNATIONAL BOUNDARY
NATIONAL PARK

# THE UPPER RIVER

*Twenty kilometres from its source the Zambezi is an attractive highland brook.*

# THE SOURCE

## MWINILUNGA

*Mike Coppinger*

IT IS ALMOST AS IF THE MAP has been drawn specifically to allow the country of Zambia to be the cradle of the mighty river that gives the nation its name. A thin finger of Zambian territory stretches north, separating Angola and Zaïre and claiming the hills in which the Zambezi is born.

In these uplands at latitude 11°22′S and longitude 24°18′E a gentle valley, clothed in dense Miombo (*Brachystegia*) woodland, slopes away to the north-east from the region's highest point at 1 454 metres above sea level. A clearing in the woodland is carpeted by a metre-deep layer of the orange, yellow and green leaves of Wild Ginger. The lower margin of the clearing is abruptly delineated by dense riverine forest filling the valley floor.

Within the forest a soft mat of damp, decaying leaves surrounds sturdy moss-covered tree trunks which support the lofty canopy. For a few hundred metres below the clearing a small stream gurgles just beneath the ground, bubbling up occasionally through twisted roots and forming a few small pools on the surface. Ultimately, it emerges through the roots of one of the giant evergreens to continue its journey above ground. The Zambezi is born. Developing a power sometimes deep, resolute and deliberate, sometimes exploding in white fury, this flow is destined to stamp its authority across the African continent before finally surrendering its life-giving bounty to the Indian Ocean 2 700 kilometres away.

The infant river sees very little daylight, as only a few rays of sun penetrate the green foliage to glint off ubiquitous cobwebs and highlight the

colours of their leggy custodians. Over the first 30 kilometres of its course the shallow stream in places reaches a width of 10 metres, its banks decorated with ferns and cycads. Groups of butterflies colour the scene as they flutter through patches of sunlight. The fringing belt of forest is continuous, if narrow, frequently bordered on the outside by dambos – marshy areas covered in thick green grass up to a metre high. The dambos are often fringed by *Hyparrhenia* grass easily tall enough to dwarf a man.

Over this distance the Zambezi flows northwards through countryside which is dominated by *Brachystegia* woodland, the vegetation type which dominates the central African highveld. It is characterized by attractive, flat-topped trees noted for the striking colours of the young foliage produced during the spring flush. Here the trees are larger and more closely ranked than is usual. A few kilometres to the east the watercourse is flanked by a ridge of land which separates the Zambezi from another major African river basin, the Zaïre. Along this ridge the woodland is interspersed with 'watershed plains' – vast areas of golden grassland which straddle the high ground. The area's altitude and an average annual rainfall of 1 400 millimetres combine to form extensive marshy areas fringing the plains. Rivulets from the marshes drain down the western slopes, nourishing mushitus – narrow strips of dense evergreen forest – as they augment the parent stream.

The Zambezi curves to the west and skirts around Kalene Hill, splashing over a series of beautiful rapids as it heads towards Angola. After 70 kilometres of life southern Africa's largest river has attained a breadth of 25 metres where it leaves the country of its birth.

When we drove north from Mwinilunga Boma towards the source of the great river in May 1987 we felt as if we were experiencing a taste of Africa as it was in decades gone by. A sandy, pot-holed dirt track guided us

---

LEFT *A* Brachystegia-*clothed hillside in Zambia's Mwinilunga district is cut by a valley crowded with giant evergreens. In the damp, shady heart of the forest the infant Zambezi gurgles through the roots of the trees.*
ABOVE *Watershed plains separate the Zambezi and Zaïre Rivers and drain into both.*

between tall, proud *Brachystegia* trees which formed an almost closed canopy high above our heads. We passed neat, colourfully plastered groups of African huts and crossed numerous fast-flowing, bouncing streams. This felt like a part of Africa where nature had not been subdued by technology.

We followed an old bush path to the top of Kalene Hill, which stands out above the surrounding countryside, offering a panoramic view of three countries. This was the site of the first Christian mission in the territory. The hill was initially noted by the missionary Frederick Arnot and the station was established by Dr Walter Fisher in 1906.

The mission has now moved to lower ground and the ruins of the original establishment are overrun by indigenous vegetation. A set of steps laid by Arnot can still be identified, and the thick clay brick walls of the church stand out defiantly amongst the trees and scrub. We picked our way through the bush and rubble to perch insignificantly on one of a jumble of massive grey boulders clinging to the north facing lip of the hill. An escarpment stretched away to the west into Angolan territory while in front of us the slope dropped to woodland extending across the Zambian border into Zaïre. Heavy black clouds of an unseasonal storm rolled ominously along the face of the hillside towards us. In the evening light, subdued by the gloom of the threatening clouds, we could still discern a smudge of darker greenery winding through the woodland. This was the tell-tale trail of the young Zambezi stream.

The first few drops of rain reached us and spattered on the graves of Dr and Mrs Walter Fisher 20 metres down the slope. Feeling the excitement that comes inevitably with the smell of wet African soil we reflected that the Fishers had themselves spent many hours where we now sat. When they arrived in the early 1900s the slave trade still afflicted the area and the resident Lunda tribespeople lived in abject fear of raids by more aggressive neighbours like the Chokwe. To avoid detection the local people lived in temporary dwellings deep in the forest. Their transient lifestyle precluded development of any significant form of agriculture, making them dependent on hunting and gathering wild fruits and plants. Thus it was very difficult for the missionaries to make contact with their subjects. Dr Fisher's solution was to watch from his vantage point on Kalene Hill for the smoke of cooking fires, take a compass bearing and set off across country in the direction of his target. Invariably his appearance in a village caused panic and precipitated a wholesale stampede of the inhabitants into the bush.

He used medicine as his tool to win the people's confidence – earning the name Ndotolu (doctor) – and finally gained acceptance with a successful cataract operation on Chieftainess Nyakaseya. It is unusual in African society for a woman to be eligible for the status of 'chief' and this situation is

LEFT *A young mother of the Lunda tribe pauses on her way to wash clothes in a small stream that rapidly becomes southern Africa's greatest river.*
OVERLEAF *After 40 kilometres the Zambezi stream creates an impressive spectacle as it bounces and slides down the 'Zambezi Rapids' north of Kalene Hill.*

indicative of the Lunda's origins. The tribe migrated south from the Kola kingdom of Zaïre in the eighteenth century and its people today are spread through north-western Zambia, eastern Angola and southern Zaïre. Colonial partitioning of territory has eroded the traditional tribal structure and the Lunda in Zambia now pay only token homage to the Paramount Chief, Mwata-Yamvwa, in Zaïre.

A number of tribes of Kola ancestry follow rules of matrilineal descent and allow female chiefs. It is significant that when the Paramount Chief in later years wished to acknowledge the Lunda's esteem for the Fisher family, he chose to award chieftainship to a woman, Mrs Singleton Fisher.

Ndotolu's mission station of sun-dried brick buildings became a catalyst for change. The people adopted his building techniques and established permanent villages; the sick came from far and wide to benefit from his medical services. For the missionaries Kalene was a place of extreme isolation. In the early years the only access to the outside world was by foot to the west coast, thence by boat to England. Caravans served by hundreds of porters marched 1 500 kilometres across the breadth of Angola to reach the sea. The loads carried by the porters included the women and children of the party. The ladies were hoisted in hammocks strung on poles, while the children were shielded from the African environment in 'meat safes' — boxes constructed of wood and wire mesh attached to poles which rested on the sturdy shoulders of the porters.

Dr Fisher's descendants are still in the area and run Hillwood farm, which supplies the mission and constitutes the commercial heart of the district. The grassy dambos, mushitus and woodland of Hillwood are threaded together by the Sakeji River, the first substantial tributary of the Zambezi.

In the 80 years since Dr Fisher's arrival in the district things have changed considerably. However, we were reminded of his early experiences with the local people one day when we were looking for birds in a tropical forest near the Lisombo stream. Sitting in a clearing, scanning the trees through our binoculars, we were startled by a sudden eruption of sound. The drumming of stampeding feet, the crack of breaking branches and the frantic rustle of disturbed foliage provided the soundtrack to a scene of sheer panic. We had surprised a party of Angolan refugees stealing across the border.

The Angolans are now fleeing from civil war instead of from slave traders. Refugees also come from Zaïre and at the time of our visit there was thought to be one refugee for every two permanent inhabitants in the region north of Mwinilunga Boma.

The productivity of the people has not matched their increase in numbers. The resilient cassava (manioc) crop is grown as the staple food, while every group of huts is surrounded by a fertile grove of banana trees. It is a legacy of the Lunda's migratory hunter-gatherer background that they do not keep cattle, or any other significant livestock. With the increase in population, hunting has led to the virtual extermination of most large mammals. A shortage of meat is now a major problem in the lives of the people, whose language even contains a specific word for 'meat hunger'.

Hillwood farm constitutes the only refuge for remaining game in the vicinity of the Zambezi. Included amongst the wildlife on the farm are a handful of sitatunga, a rare antelope specific to marshy country.

The Lunda are expert trappers and they now concentrate on snaring birds. In addition to setting ingenious and effective traps in strategic places, every man and boy carries a catapult in case of a chance to add a bit of 'relish' to the evening meal. The Mwinilunga district is known to have a particularly interesting bird population, situated as it is on the fringe of the equatorial zone. However, although the diversity of species still exists, the predation has obviously taken a toll as one has to search hard to find birds.

The method of harvesting caterpillars further illustrates the people's failure to perceive that mother nature is not a limitless source of bounty. At certain times of the year some trees become infested by these insects, which can be preserved and stored as a food supply. The technique for collecting them is simply to chop down the trees.

With the pressure on the land, traditional food resources are almost exhausted and new methods are needed to sustain the current population and to preserve the environment. As in many parts of Third World Africa, the only hope of such techniques being implemented appears to be via the involvement of foreign organizations. The large refugee population coupled with a high incidence of protein malnutrition brought the Mwinilunga district into consideration for international aid. In 1983 a fish farming project was initiated with the aim of capitalizing on the abundance of water.

At the time of our visit this scheme had yet to make really meaningful progress. Initial problems in implementation were reasonably predictable. Farmers were reluctant to feed the fish since those in the rivers feed themselves. In cropping there was a tendency to extract the largest fish, thus causing genetic degeneration.

More substantial hurdles threatening the success of the project are of a psychological nature. The farmers have been reluctant to accept responsibility for their own circumstances. Furthermore the ever present shadow of witchcraft has to be contended with. A successful African farmer runs a great risk of incurring the jealousy of his neighbours. The witchdoctor is often invoked to punish anybody guilty of rising above the common level. Productive farmers have been known to crop their fish secretly at night to avoid recognition of their success. If these problems can be overcome fish farming could make a substantial contribution to satisfying the local demand for protein.

When we had completed our study of the area we drove south back to Mwinilunga Boma along the magnificent *Brachystegia* avenue. Towards us through the dappled sunlight strode a man carrying a bow and arrow. Barely acknowledging our presence he glanced at us in passing, his expression epitomizing the raw splendour of ancient Africa which still characterizes this part of the continent. However we had learned that the balance between man and nature was now delicately poised, and we wondered where the hunter's journey would end.

# GOD'S HIGHWAY

## CHAVUMA TO ZAMBEZI

*Mike Coppinger*

THE WAR IN ANGOLA prevented us from pursuing the Zambezi through that country. Instead we followed the West Lunga and Kabompo tributaries and renewed our association with the Zambezi where it returns to Zambian soil at Chavuma. The river had grown considerably in stature since our previous view of it, 300 kilometres upstream, and it creates a powerful spectacle as it surges over the Chavuma Falls. The falls would actually be more appropriately described as a rapid, as the river is compressed into a narrow rock-walled passage, then plunges down a drop of several metres. The cascade forms a 'hole' in the middle of the flow which is backed up by a formidable stopper wave. Below the rapid the river forms a wide pool before resuming its passage, and across here a motorized pontoon provides vehicle access to the west bank.

The escarpment which we previously observed spreading west from Kalene terminates here on the east bank and the hill closest to the river is the site of another CMML (Christian Missions In Many Lands) mission. As was the case with Kalene, the location on a hilltop was chosen to alleviate the malaria problem. Access and water supply are difficulties which are inherent in this choice.

The mission is the largest establishment in Chavuma, but there are a number of other buildings sprawled out over a wide area. Administratively Chavuma is classified as a sub-boma, falling under the jurisdiction of Zambezi Boma, some 100 kilometres to the south. The administrative office is situated at the base of the hill, not far from the falls. Nearby is a general store and small shops and simple houses are scattered for about six kilometres along the sandy Zambezi road. A side road leads to the Angolan border post where the customs, police and immigration are based.

One of the colonial governors visiting the place once described Chavuma as 'the most remote corner of the British Empire'. Of course it is no longer a part of the empire, but it is still a remarkably isolated settlement. It is tucked away in a forgotten nook of the country and is not on the way to anywhere – particularly while hostilities prevail in Angola. There is no telephone, but the post office is serviced by a yellow Land-Rover which travels up from Zambezi – with a little post box fixed on the back to pick up any passing trade.

We had first-hand experience of the bus service which operates rather haphazardly between Zambezi and Chavuma a couple of times a week. Trying to catch the bus from Zambezi we spent two days sitting in the dust at the 'bus terminus'. We were dismayed to learn that some hopeful passengers had been waiting three weeks for a bus to Kitwe, even staying overnight to keep their places in the queue. We were thus thankful when our bus eventually pulled up, but had to fight for our rights when all semblance of order collapsed as people stormed the vehicle. Our journey only commenced once every conceivable space had been crammed with some form of cargo.

In colonial times a barge provided an infrequent transport service from Victoria Falls all the way up to Chavuma. Before the building of roads this was in fact the only recognized transport route to the outside world. The frustrations of being at the end of the line were epitomized by the experiences of a Chavuma District Commissioner who had a taste for Scotch whisky. He regularly ordered a case of the finest Scotch to be sent up on the

LEFT *Winter nights on the Upper Zambezi often bring temperatures close to freezing. Day then breaks through shrouds of mist.*
ABOVE *The Upper Zambezi is remote from modern technology.*

barge, and just as regularly the case would arrive a few months later with no bottles, only IOU's from officials further downstream!

The Zambezi we had explored in the Mwinilunga district had not been large enough to support boat travel, but here the river presented itself as a highway. We concluded that the only practical way for us to study its passage was to adopt the local technique of using a dug-out canoe. These craft have been used since time immemorial to ply the waterway. Early this century the Luvale people of this district used to trade with the Lozis, who lived on the floodplain a couple of hundred kilometres to the south. The Lozis provided a ready market for products of the forest such as canoes, bark ropes, axe and hoe handles, mortars and pestles and house building materials. The Luvale paddled these goods downstream and exchanged canoes and their contents for cattle, which they would then walk back. Towards the middle of the century the trade shifted more towards supplying the Lozis with cassava meal. Nowadays, however, it appears that this merchant trade on the river has virtually dried up. Any produce that the Luvale have for export tends to be shipped by road to the cities of central Zambia.

We were surprised to find that the Chavuma boatmen are now not accustomed to travel even as far astream as Zambezi Boma. Nonetheless after a certain amount of negotiation we secured the services of two able-bodied paddlers, James and Simeon, and a sturdy canoe to take us downstream. Preparations complete, it was with a tingle of excitement that we slipped

ABOVE *The only common form of transport on the river's upper reaches is the dug-out canoe. These craftsmen are fashioning boats from the trunks of False mopane* (Guibourtia coleosperma) *trees. Their work will be completed in about 14 days.*
ABOVE RIGHT *Children in rural communities share in the burden of the family's subsistence from an early age. Fish traps are most effective when laid in swift-flowing waters.*

away from the shore with the surging sound of the Chavuma Falls behind us and the mystery of a new Zambezi stretch ahead. In the course of our journey we were to see nothing to indicate that man had ever interfered with the working of this waterway. The flow was never impeded or diverted, there were no permanent man-made structures visible from the river, with the exceptions of Chinyingi Mission and Zambezi Boma, and we didn't encounter evidence of any form of pollution. On rare occasions we saw the huts of villages or met local fishermen in their canoes. Two or three times we saw cattle browsing near the water's edge.

We found ourselves travelling on a 200-metre wide band of smooth blue water flowing steadily through a flat countryside of Kalahari sand. The vegetation pattern was unchanging. Forming a continuous fringe along the shore and encroaching into the water is a specialized form of the Water-berry tree (*Syzygium guineense*). The tree has a creamy-grey bark and tends to grow at an angle, leaning out from the bank, drooping its branches and

dark green leaves over the water. It is able to hold its precarious position against the current by virtue of its well-adapted root system. An extensive network of ground roots, often partially exposed, spread out to anchor the plant. In addition, the trunk and branches leaning over the flow drop aerial roots of varying thickness. Tipped with fine hairs they give a brush-like impression when exposed above the water. Some of these roots reach the river bed and serve as additional stabilizers.

These *Syzygium* trees obviously need to be well secured as considerable fluctuations in water level occur. As we travelled downstream in the month of June, a high-water mark could be distinctly seen at least six metres above the current level of the river. This means that during the wet season the trees are completely submerged. The area behind the *Syzygium* fringe and leading up to the high-water mark is occupied for the most part by sparsely vegetated sloping banks. Atop these banks Kalahari woodland, alternating with short grassland, stretches away to the horizon. The grasslands become inundated during the wet season to form dambos, some of which remain permanently wet. We heard from the local people of the navigational difficulties encountered during the flood season when the main channel loses its clear definition and the river spreads into the surrounding plains.

Prominent tree species in the Kalahari woodland are Mukwa (*Pterocarpus angolensis*), Pod mahogany (*Afzelia quanzensis*), False mopane (*Guibourtia coleosperma*) and the Tick tree (*Sterculia africana*). One also encounters occa-

sional specimens of *Garcinea livingstonei*, which is a common constituent of riparian forest along the Zambezi at lower altitudes.

The weather while we were on the river was remarkably consistent. When the sun rose at 07h00 it was the coldest time, with the temperature dropping as low as one degree Celsius, and the river was shrouded in mist. By 09h00 the day was beautifully warm and the clear blue skies never harboured a cloud. A gentle cooling breeze blew from the east during the midday hours. In this setting we made our way leisurely downstream to the rhythmic sound of splashing paddles and the occasional chatter and song of the paddlers. As along most parts of the Zambezi our passage was watched by Greenbacked Heron which, perched on overhanging branches, would give a sharp croak and fly off along the bank when we got too close. Other notable bird species which we observed in the *Syzygium* were Wattle-eyed Flycatcher and Olive Woodpecker. We also had splendid views of Ross' Lourie, a dazzling violet Turaco with crimson wings and a yellow beak. However the consistent nature of the vegetation means that there isn't a great variety of bird life to be seen.

A feature of the river at this time of year are the extensive white beaches which tend to form on the inside curves of the river, often opposite a low clay cliff on the outside bend. On our second afternoon out we had just passed a village where James and Simeon had managed to purchase some live relish in the form of a chicken, when we came upon a beautiful exam-

ABOVE *Little has changed in the vicinity of Chitokoloki since missionary Frederick Arnot explored the area in the early 1900s.*
RIGHT *The Zambezi, running south from Chavuma to Katima Mulilo, effectively isolates the western strip of Zambia from the rest of the country. Access to the west bank is afforded only by a few pontoons and this ingenious footbridge that crosses the river at Chinyingi.*

ple of one such formation. We had little hesitation in deciding to make an early camp to enable us to exploit the photographic potential of the setting, and to give the paddlers time to give their full attention to our temporary travelling companion.

The beach was more than a kilometre long and up to 150 metres in width. The clean sand squeaked loudly as we walked on it, and our bare footprints only accentuated the natural purity of the scene. The sun sank towards the horizon directly upstream, casting long shadows which high-lighted the precise wind- and water-formed patterns in the sand. As the light faded I ambled up to the tree line, where we had cleared a camp site. A few feathers lying on the ground and Simeon's preoccupied expression as he tended the fire confirmed that the complement of our travelling party had been reduced once again to four.

James and Simeon were not well equipped for our expedition. In our negotiations it had been established that they were to provide their own rations and bedding. The Africans in these parts do not enjoy a great variety of food. Meals consist of a large portion of nshima – a meal made from crushed maize or cassava cooked with water to form a heavy dough – eaten with 'relish'. The relish is all-important and preferably contains meat, but may consist of fish and can include vegetables. Our paddlers had com-

menced the journey with only a small supply of mealie meal – which we had supplemented from our stocks – and they acquired relish en route. In the bedding department they had nothing at all. James explained that he had a wife with whom he shared a single blanket, therefore he had nothing he could take away with him. Even we in our sleeping bags were not very comfortable with the cold and heavy dew at night. Our colleagues simply built a semi-circular barricade of branches around the fire to trap some warmth and lay down in their clothes. Simeon's trousers were cut off above the knee and he wore no shoes. We were not at all surprised when they commented one morning that they had suffered from 'coldness' and also 'mosquitoeness'.

On the fourth day we encountered the most unusual sight on this stretch of river. At Chinyingi mission the Catholic Capuchin Friars have built a suspension footbridge, modelled on San Francisco's Golden Gate, across the Zambezi. There are bitter-sweet stories associated with this construction. When the mission was established in 1954 the Lunda chief on the more accessible east bank refused to approve a site for the mission. Sanction was, however, received from the Luvale chief on the west bank and the mission

ABOVE *The river flowing through remote western Zambia has not been subjected to any form of major development or pollution.*
OPPOSITE *The view from Chinyingi mission is typical of the Zambezi's upper reaches.* Syzygium *trees line a tranquil, meandering passage through flat Kalahari sand country.*

was duly established there, with the contingent transport problems. A pontoon was installed for ferrying motor vehicles, and a small boat was used for transporting passengers.

One moonless night Father Rock set out on an errand of mercy. He returned to the Zambezi with a moribund patient and a full boatload of relatives. No-one has ever established what happened out on the river that night, but the crossing was never completed. The craft foundered and Father Rock along with a number of passengers were drowned. In response to this tragedy Brother Crispin set about construction of the suspension bridge. With great resourcefulness and at minimal cost to the mission he erected the only bridge to span the Zambezi on its 800-kilometre passage between the Angolan border and the Victoria Falls.

We enjoyed tremendous hospitality from the missionaries at Chinyingi when we spent a night there. Father Luke recounted a more light-hearted tale concerning the structure. Before being stationed at the mission Luke visited the establishment one night with Father Charlie, a formidable figure of a man who weighed more than 150 kilograms. It was pitch dark when Father Charlie set off across the footbridge carrying a case of beer. After a short while Luke, waiting on the far bank, heard sounds of distress emanating from the darkness. Gingerly he ventured out onto the swaying cableway to check that his friend had not come to harm. When he was over mid-stream his torch beam fell upon the case of beer lying undamaged and unattended next to a gaping hole in the floorboards. The planks had proved unequal to the challenge of supporting Father Charlie's bulk and he had plummeted 15 metres into the swirling Zambezi. Happily he made his way to shore unscathed, if somewhat disorientated!

One day's paddling from Chinyingi brought us to our destination – Zambezi Boma. James and Simeon were clearly proud of their achievement as they described our expedition to bystanders while we disembarked. We paid them off and they began preparations for the return journey. For Jumbo and me it had been a unique experience, the only disappointing aspect being the lack of wildlife, particularly that we didn't see a single hippo or crocodile. We did see a few otters and a number of interesting bird species.

In Zambezi we had the good fortune to be befriended by Dave and Grace Croudace, people who have dedicated their life's work to the people in this district. Grace's father founded the Chavuma mission, where she was raised, and Dave came to western Zambia from Southern Rhodesia to pursue his missionary career – and later Grace! Their fellowship and home cooking fortified us for the travels that lay ahead.

Although Chavuma district is one of the more densely populated parts of Zambia, which is not a very heavily peopled country, the population doesn't appear to place pressure on the river. The extensive seasonal flooding plays a part in keeping permanent settlement away from the main stream. High rainfall, coupled with the flooding, also ensures a good general water supply which affords the people some latitude in their choice of domicile. We have already seen that the waterway is put to limited use for commercial travel and it provides a livelihood to many people through fishing.

The prevalent tribe in the area are the Luvale, who share a common ancestry with the Lunda, a significant number of whom also live here. The Luvale are more river-orientated than the Lunda and in the past were more dominant than their cousins. They tended more to barter with the slave traders rather than be preyed upon and were also successful in repulsing an invasion from the south by the Kololo, who had subdued the Lozi.

The Luvale suffered a number of setbacks with the advent of colonialism. Initially the British, via the British South Africa Company, concluded an agreement with Lewanika, King of the Lozis, which gave them certain rights in the territory of his tribe. The British counted the Luvale as subjects of the Lozi, which was hotly disputed by the Luvale. It was only in 1941

that a long-standing inquiry, the MacDonnel Commission, ruled in favour of Luvale sovereignty and the distinct Balovale (now Zambezi) administrative authority was established.

The British made a further error of interpretation in 1948 when they ruled that the Zambezi River constituted a dividing line between the Luvale to the west and the Lunda to the east. The local Lunda chief was thus recognized as chief of the Chavuma area. In reality the people were of both tribes and the chief soon left because he was not able to govern effectively. Eventually a compromise solution was sought by appealing to the tribes' common ancestry. Both peoples recognized Mwata-Yamvwa as their Paramount Chief, so the case was presented to him and he actually visited Chavuma in 1957. His decision was to appoint his daughter, Luweji, as chief. Unfortunately her capabilities did not match the requirements of the situation and she returned to Zaïre after a few years. The people of Chavuma were thus left without a chief and that condition persists today, with the matter having been passed to the Zambian government for resolution. In the meantime one Luvale man has described their situation: 'Without a chief we are like fish in a pool to be caught by anyone.'

# CROSSROADS

## ZAMBEZI TO LUKULU

*Mike Coppinger*

LUKULU IS MORE READILY accessible by road than either Zambezi town or Chavuma. We were thus able to set up a base there with all our equipment, thanks to the kind help of the Catholics at Sancta Maria mission. From this base we conducted sorties in our motorized rubber dinghy as far upstream as Zambezi – 110 kilometres away – where our canoeing adventure had ended. The longest such boating safari was a seven and a half day trip. Our payload included the standard 20-litre petrol tank, two 20-litre jerrycans, our two camera boxes, a bag of boat accessories, food trunk, bucket, two kit bags, three fishing rods and tackle, two camping mattresses, tent and two small cooler bags packed with such scientific items as thermometer, vernier scale, etc.

Meeting up again with the Croudaces at the northern limit of our excursions had a positive impact on both our morale and our larder. Travelling south from Zambezi at idling or drifting pace we found the riverscape almost monotonous. As is the case upstream, *Syzygium* dominates the shoreline. It occurred to us that perhaps these trees are responsible for the stability of the river's channel. Even though extensive annual flooding takes place the channel was exactly as marked on our map, printed in 1966. This is in sharp contrast to the situation on the Middle Zambezi, where the river continually eats away at its banks, or on the Luangwa tributary, which is constantly changing course and creating oxbow lagoons.

The *Syzygium* was not very active with bird life, probably because it was not in flower or fruit at the time of our passage. Also, being separated from the dry woodland by the flood zone, the normal woodland species don't seem to have any reason for coming across. The trees do provide vantage positions from which birds can perch over the water – a facility which is utilized mainly by Greenbacked Heron and kingfishers. Small fish were visible in abundance close to shore. We also saw a number of small tiger fish and frequently heard the splashes of their feeding.

We became more aware of *Phragmites* reeds mingling with the *Syzygium*. These reeds form a thin, usually see-through strip along the water's edge. This vegetation is not thick enough to create a solid or matted surface on the water in which shy, lurking birds can take refuge. Furthermore, as the reeds occupy the zone where water meets land they possibly eliminate the use of the shoreline by waders – those birds who forage on the wet sandflats. In the few places along the riverbank where the *Phragmites* forms a dense bed, weaver birds occur.

The sandbank pattern which became so familiar on the Chavuma-Zambezi section is a diminishing characteristic which disappears entirely downstream of Chitokoloki. The phasing out of the sandbanks coincides with the appearance of rock on the river bed, sometimes protruding above the surface of the water. This rock occurs in belts spanning the river, but does not form a feature in the surrounding countryside.

The river continues to traverse Kalahari sand country. The water is clear and doesn't carry much material in suspension. The sandy bed, when it can be seen, is usually bare. Periodically, at the meeting of underground tributaries, small stretches of the bank are of clay. In these instances the bank forms a cliff some metres high which is perpetually damp, with constant seepage taking place. These banks support attractive small feathery ferns.

LEFT *The Zambezi gathers the flow of a number of major tributaries, each with a unique character derived ultimately from the nature of the soils it traverses. The sandy base of the Lunguevungu results in clear water and sparsely vegetated banks.* ABOVE *Sand banks are the preferred habitat of many bird species.*

37

Apart from birds, leguaans were the animals we saw most often, generally being flushed from the banks or from overhanging branches in the *Syzygium*. We encountered one hippo and no crocodiles. The hippo slipped silently into the water from riverine bush as we passed by. We didn't see him surface again and this furtive behaviour gave us the distinct impression that he was a hunted animal.

Suddenly one's senses start to tingle with the sensations of a different kind of Africa. Is there a different smell in the air? Is there somehow more activity? There is definitely an atmosphere of expectancy and impending change. One notices that on the east bank the *Phragmites* disappears to be replaced by a dark green emergent reed which encroaches well into the stream. Closer to the shore one sees floating vegetation for the first time and on the bank the monotony of the *Syzygium* is broken by the infusion of new lush riverine trees and creepers. On the west bank the normal sandy inundation zone disappears to be replaced by a much higher ridge of dry woodland rising steeply from the water's edge.

One has just taken stock of these changes when the east bank opens up to greet a vast body of water almost as wide as the Zambezi itself. The Kabompo has joined forces with its illustrious companion. We encountered four hippos right at the confluence behaving as hippos should – wallowing in midstream with just the tops of their heads protruding above the surface, ears flicking to chase away the flies and little piggy eyes peering over dilated nostrils. A flock of 20 Carmine Bee-eaters sparkled overhead, while higher up a whitebacked Bateleur eagle soared effortlessly. The call of the African Fish Eagle echoed over the Kabompo waters.

The vibrancy of this new world drew us irresistibly up the tributary. Instead of sand the banks are of sticky dark clay, and slimy, hair-like green weed covers the river bed. The water also appears green and there is a considerable amount of the plant in suspension. The banks of the Kabompo are mostly covered in dense, impenetrable vegetation. In places this consists of thick beds of *Phragmites*, on a scale not seen on the Zambezi. The reeds are sometimes mixed with other aquatic plants and these beds definitely constitute a haven for birds. Spottedbacked and Spectacled Weaver can be seen busily constructing their neat nests, while the frequent intriguing growl of Black Crake betrays the presence of inhabitants in secret places.

Alternatively the *Phragmites* gives way to riparian forest. *Syzygium* is a component of this forest, but is not as dominant as on the Zambezi. A mix of other trees is present including *Acacia sieberana* and *Acacia albida*, which is so prominent in the Middle Zambezi. A generally tropical impression is reinforced by creepers entwined in the trees, monkeys peering down from the branches and palm trees in the background. The *Syzygium* trees differ from their Zambezi counterparts in that they lack aerial roots. Also, although still overhanging the water, they have a tendency to grow straighter and taller. Possibly the explanation lies in the fact that these trees are rooted in clay as opposed to sand and are not subjected to quite as drastic flooding.

In the woodland away from the river we recorded our most northerly sightings of the Sausage tree (*Kigelia africana*) and Rain tree (*Lonchocarpus capassa*), which are common further south.

In addition to the more prolific bird life, over the 30-kilometre stretch of Kabompo travelled, we had several sightings of crocodiles and heard hippos, without seeing them. The presence of the majestic African Fish Eagle adds a special touch of splendour. This bird is widespread on the Zambezi downstream from this point and we have been unable to find any explanation for its absence further north.

In places along the Kabompo people cultivate fields right on the water's edge, which does not happen on the Zambezi. Bush clearing is obviously a substantial effort, but must be worth the benefits yielded by the fertile clay. The damp soil is also more easily worked than that of the hard, dry ground further inland.

When we returned to the confluence I felt compelled to take advantage of the height afforded by the ridge on the west bank to photograph the meeting of these two giant African rivers. Accordingly I got Jumbo to drop me off while he explored other areas. Climbing the ridge was more arduous than I had anticipated and when I reached the top I found that I still had to climb a tree and remove a few branches to get a clear view. This was done in the irritating company of a cloud of mopane flies – tiny stingless bees which crawl up one's nose and into one's eyes in search of moisture. I was ultimately rewarded with a good view of the confluence and took some photographs. Spotting a lone boatman paddling his canoe down the near bank I decided he would provide the perfect foreground for my shot. I duly leaned out from my perch and shouted at him to 'please move further out into the stream so that I can take a photograph'. He had probably not seen many white men in his time and certainly none in this area. Thus when he looked up to see a mukuwa (white man) hanging from a branch 20 metres above him shouting and waving, the disbelief was clearly registered on his face. One hard look was all he needed, then he put his head down and paddled purposefully out of my sight!

The Kabompo's influence extends for some distance down the east bank of the parent river, with the soil and vegetation types gradually reverting to the more standard Zambezi pattern. However, no sooner has the tropical excitement of the Kabompo started to wane than one becomes aware of changes on the west bank. The ridge and its mopane flies have been left behind, the hinterland has flattened out and is populated by palm trees (*Hyphaene benguellensis*) in a profusion not yet encountered on the Zambezi.

Just 25 kilometres downstream of the Kabompo confluence and from the opposite side of the compass, the Zambezi receives the waters of another major African river, the Lunguevungu. Whereas the Kabompo's course traverses fertile soils, the Lunguevungu rises in the Angolan highlands and runs

*The African Jacana derives its common name of 'lilytrotter' from its ability to walk upon floating vegetation. Its exceptionally long toes enable it to spread its weight across supporting plants as it forages among the leaves.*

LEFT *Along parts of the Zambezi in western Zambia where trees are scarce the stately African Fish Eagle often has to settle for a lowly perch.*
ABOVE *The Kabompo supports more luxurious growth than the adjoining Zambezi. The more fertile nature of the smaller river is illustrated by a greater diversity and abundance of wildlife.*

for most of its length over relatively sterile sands in western Zambia. The different circumstances create two rivers of vastly differing character.

Boating up the Lunguevungu we found the water to be a golden brown colour, and to navigate successfully we had to follow the main channel around shallowly submerged sandbanks. The river bed is white sand often mixed with a bit of clay which gives it a firm texture. We did not encounter squeaky, bleached beaches of the kind found further up the Zambezi. The banks of the Lunguevungu are nowhere high – seldom exceeding two metres – and consist of alternate stretches of low sand cliffs and emergent aquatic vegetation. *Phragmites* is once again the dominant aquatic growth but is interspersed with Papyrus. In some places sand banks were exposed and they must become an increasingly prominent feature as the water level of the river drops.

Particularly in the five kilometres closest to the confluence the river twists and turns and there is evidence that it has often changed its course. It is interesting to note that *Syzygium* is sparsely distributed, tending to concentrate in dense forest patches around islands, inlets and old river courses. The inlets support floating vegetation such as waterlilies so it is not surprising that investigation yields bird species like Pygmy Goose and African Jacana. The Jacana is often referred to as a 'lilytrotter' because of the way it walks or

41

runs over floating plants in search of food. The shy and unobtrusive Pygmy Goose, which feeds almost exclusively on the ripe seeds of waterlilies, looks like a precisely patterned and carved little wooden duck.

Away from the river, particularly on the southern bank, short grassland predominates, with Kalahari woodland appearing in scattered patches. There is no human habitation within 15 kilometres of the confluence, presumably because of the susceptibility to flooding. The sparse population is congregated on higher land afforded by a series of ridges running away from the river in a north-easterly direction, the villages being characterized by dense groves of mango trees. People we met on the river in their dugouts were either fishing or transporting loads of mealie meal up from Lukulu.

Two snorting hippos greeted us at the confluence and on a number of occasions we saw hippo tracks upstream. We also got close to a large croco-

*Extensive sandbanks exposed on the Lunguevungu tributary and Zambezi flood-plain during the dry season constitute a prolific nursery for ground-nesting birds. Typical amongst these are the African Skimmer (ABOVE) which excavates a neat conical scrape on the beach in which it lays its eggs. Parents constantly shade their clutches from the summer heat. The Redwinged Pratincole (RIGHT) prefers to use an indentation such as an animal's footprint for a nest. The chick hatches after some 18 days of incubation and soon leaves the nest to seek cover in ground vegetation.*

dile lying on a low grassy bank, but the only other animals we observed apart from birds were otters and leguaans. The avifauna consisted mainly of those species utilising the sand banks and cliffs. The birds which inhabit sand cliffs include the river's most colourful species, namely bee-eaters and kingfishers. We suspected that the Carmine Bee-eaters sighted over the

Kabompo confluence had originated from the Lunguevungu, but we failed to discover a colony. However, we did spend some time observing and photographing equally spectacular Whitefronted Bee-eaters, who sometimes use the same nesting holes as the Carmines but at a different time of year. The nest is an inclined burrow up to about a metre long. A colony can consist of hundreds of individuals, and their squeaky, unmelodious voices combine to make quite a din, particularly in the evenings when they all gather at the nesting site.

Also of special interest to us was the presence in some numbers of African Skimmer, an intra-African migrant confined to large bodies of water and seldom occurring south of the Zambezi. They were breeding on the Lunguevungu and we recorded eight clutches of eggs on the flat sandbanks. This was an indication of things to come further downstream.

Having completed our upstream explorations we returned to our Lukulu base. The settlement is located on the Zambezi's east bank just downstream of the Lunguevungu confluence. We discovered that while we had been out on the river two boys swimming near the mission had been attacked by a crocodile. The crocodile took one of them and the other drowned in panic. The tragedy was a reminder of the respect that the river warrants.

The merging of these three rivers in such proximity provided us with a very graphic ecology lesson. We saw an illustration of how each river's origins influenced its fertility and how that was portrayed in the variety and quantity of plant and animal life supported.

From our base at Sancta Maria mission we were now well situated to venture south. When we did so we were to witness yet another dramatic change in environment.

# BULOZI

## THE ZAMBEZI FLOODPLAIN

*Mike Coppinger*

BULOZI – THE ZAMBEZI FLOODPLAIN: the concept was so evocative that 'butterflies' of anticipation fluttered through my stomach. Would we make the most of our single opportunity to explore this unique phenomenon? Would our boat continue to respond faithfully to the demands made of it in these remote backwaters? Could we elude the perpetual security threat posed by over-zealous militia?

After two busy days at the Sancta Maria Mission maintaining our boat and vehicle, catching up on book work and organizing supplies we were ready to pursue the answers to these questions.

Finally, in an atmosphere of taut expectation and with the able assistance of Bo (mister) Bill's work force, we lugged our boat and equipment from the mission buildings down the bank to the water's edge. By 10h30 preparations were complete, we bade farewell to our helpers and set course for the heart of the Lozi kingdom.

The wedge-shaped Bulozi plain is flanked by distinctive sand scarps and extends from just south of Lukulu, reaching a width of about 50 kilometres near Mongu, and tapering southwards to disappear just above the Ngonye Falls – a length of some 250 kilometres. It forms part of a major basin of sedimentation overspread by deposits of the Kalahari system, mainly in the form of sands and sandstones.

Rainfall on the upper Zambezi generally begins in November and ends in April, with the highest river flow generated in March or April. The flood-waters pour into the flat plains, which are capable of storing 8,5 billion cubic metres of water at normal annual flood levels and over 17 billion cubic metres at the peak of high floods. This dispersion of water into the surrounding countryside has the effect of delaying the flood peak by nearly a month. Thus the height of the main Zambezi flood normally arrives at Kariba about one month after the rise in water level resulting from rains in the lower catchment area. However, this regulation is accompanied by substantial losses from evaporation.

The Lozi were earlier known as the Luyi and came to the Barotse plain, as Bulozi was formerly known, from the Congo or Angola in the 1600s. In about 1830 the Kololo, a branch of the Suthu, migrated northwards, past Botswana's Lake Ngami to the Zambezi. Led by Chief Sebitwane, they conquered the Lozi and occupied most of Barotseland. Although the reign of the conquerors did not last long their language, Sikololo, became the lingua franca of the Barotse plain and has remained so to this day.

The Kololo came from the southern cattle-oriented culture and although the Lozi did keep livestock before the invasion, the tradition was strengthened. Another influence they left behind was the establishment of patrilineal descent in the royal line. The Luyi had probably been matrilineal like most people from the north.

During the time of Kololo rule a further invasion from the south was attempted by the Matabele. The insurgents were repulsed in a great victory gained by cunning. With the invading army advancing up the west bank of the Zambezi the Kololo placed a number of cattle on Mbeta Island, which lies between Senanga and Sioma. The noise made by the cattle convinced the invaders that Mbeta was the opposite bank and the army made its crossing. During the night the Kololo then succeeded in stealing their canoes,

LEFT *The Lozis are essentially river people. Their simple craft are man-powered and used primarily to transport fish to market and carry supplies, particularly maize meal, to remote villages.*
ABOVE *Tigerfish thrive on the Bulozi floodplain and are frequently netted.*

and the Matabele, being unable to swim, were stranded on the island. Once they had been sufficiently weakened by hunger the Kololo crossed and slaughtered the horde.

After the Kololo had been overthrown in 1864 Lubosi Lewanika took power and he became the most famous of the Paramount Chiefs and founder of the existing line. Lewanika was a statesman who could read the signs of the times and he reacted to colonial developments by negotiating a treaty with the British in 1890. In terms of this treaty the British South Africa Company obtained certain mining and access rights and the Lozi Kingdom was granted protectorate status which prohibited Europeans from owning land.

The Lozi's well-developed sense of identity motivated them to pursue their own sovereignty at the time of Zambian independence in 1964. However, their efforts were unsuccessful, Barotseland was renamed Western Province, and the current Litunga (king) has accepted the position of Member of the government's Central Committee.

By the evening of the first day we found ourselves 80 kilometres downstream of Lukulu when we were attracted to a sand bank which was very active with bird life. The scene was idyllic – the bank formed a wide spit between the main stream and a reed-fringed lagoon. We pitched our tent at the southern end of this pristine white beach, conceding that we were a little too close to the water for safety from crocodiles and mosquitoes, but unable to resist the beauty of the setting.

---

LEFT *On the Zambezi floodplain we savoured the feeling that man still lives in harmony with nature.*

ABOVE *Each year migrants move onto the floodplain as floodwaters recede. The floor mat will add some comfort to a temporary winter dwelling.*

As the sun dipped beneath the horizon a large-mouthed bream which some fishermen had given us sizzled in the pan. Standing barefoot in the sand I surveyed the ocean-flat horizon and was overwhelmed by the sense of freedom that emanated from the wide open spaces and the purity of the scene. The evening disappeared into a moonless night lit only by the glow of a dazzling array of stars shining out of a cloudless sky. Lying flat on our backs we studied the constellations to the accompaniment of the notes of a marimba (xylophone) wafting across from a nearby fishing village.

I favoured this style of star gazing after my experience a few weeks earlier at a safari camp on the banks of the Luangwa. I had been peering heavenwards while holding a planisphere aloft and expounding to my companions what was where in the great vault. When I took a step backwards I vanished over the three metre high river bank. Landing in a bemused heap at the bottom of the drop the only night sound I could hear was the raucous laughter of my audience. I brushed off the mud and sand but never quite recaptured my former air of authority!

This was the first of many enchanting days and nights on the floodplain. An impression constantly reinforced was that here, more than anywhere else we had been, was an atmosphere of harmony between man and nature. We felt as if we were in a supreme wilderness – yet we were seldom alone. There were more people around than we had previously encountered on the river, but they fitted into rather than dominated their environment, and moved about peacefully and unobtrusively in pursuit of their livelihood.

One evening we camped adjacent to an island which was particularly prolific in bird life, the prominent species being African Skimmers and Greyheaded Gulls. The main channel flowed between us and the island and we pitched our tent atop the 1,5 metre high river bank. The oceanic similarity was heightened during the night by the cries of the gulls which would herald the passing of fishing boats. Hearing the quiet splash of water and the gentle 'clunk' of a paddle hitting a wooden boat I would occasionally peer out of my sleeping bag. I could then make out the ghostly silhouettes of the heads and shoulders of a pair of fishermen gliding above the top of the bank.

Frequently, passing fishermen would call at our camp or we would approach them as they went about their daily tasks. One day I asked Jumbo to drop me off at Imwinda, one of the larger settlements we had encountered, as I was eager to gain some insight into village life. The settlement consisted of about 20 temporary grass huts sprawled along the edge of a lagoon. On arrival I introduced myself to the Induna, or village chief, to pay my respects and obtain his approval for my visit. He was a leper who had lost his fingers and yet was nonetheless busy repairing a fishing net. He was friendly and polite and had no objection to my presence. However, I was a curiosity and subjected to the kind of 'terrorism' one comes to expect from children in remote African villages. In no time I had an entourage of wide-eyed, semi-clad urchins who followed my every move with shouts and gales of laughter. When I swung my camera towards them some scattered in panic, but the bolder ones postured brazenly.

The village operates from April to October and owes its location to particularly good fishing in the lagoon. The Induna is subordinate to a member of the Lozi royal family who lives in a permanent village a few kilometres from the river. During the season Imwinda is used as a fishing base by people from as far afield as Zambezi and Mongu, but those who do not come from the immediate vicinity have to pay rent in money or fish.

Some of the fishermen have their wives in the village. While I was there the women were primarily engaged in brewing beer for festivities which were scheduled to take place two days hence. Two 44-gallon drums were filled to the brim with a foaming brown brew. Burning cow dung was packed around the drums and the women stirred the concoction with long poles. A grass screen sheltered the fire from the wind and also served as cover for the brewers whenever I tried to photograph them.

Before leaving the village in the evening I made the acquaintance of Beny Chitenge, who had set his four nets in the lagoon earlier in the afternoon. I arranged to go with him to check his catch in the morning. Jumbo, meanwhile, had been observing and photographing birds and had located an Avocet's nest, near which he had erected a hide for use the next day. The sun had set by the time we regrouped and we hastily set up camp on a wide sand bank across the river from Imwinda. A hippo shuffled around our tent during the night, but he had the good grace not to do any damage. It was a cool 10 °C when we crawled out of our sleeping bags well before dawn and broke camp. We boated across to Jumbo's hide and he stealthily crept inside before the Avocets had opened their eyes. As I motored across to Imwinda on the east bank the grass shacks were silhouetted against the pastel shades of the dawn sky.

Beny didn't have a hut, but he and his brother had erected a grass windbreak to provide shelter from the prevailing easterly wind. Thus protected they slept on the ground next to the fish drying rack they had made from branches. I found Beny still securely wrapped in his blanket, smilingly offering the excuse that it was cold. Together we headed out into the lagoon in his dugout and as we pulled in the nets the silvery shapes of small bream glinted in the early morning light.

Beny's daily routine had begun. Back on shore his next task was to extract his catch from the nets, cut the fish in half and lay them on the racks to sun dry for a couple of days. During this process flies swarm all over the fish, so once dried they are purified by cooking over a fire for five minutes. Thus treated the produce will last, so it is then tied in bundles for transport to market. Periodically Beny and his brother take their catch to either Mongu or Lukulu for sale. That is a two-day trip each way in the canoe.

A few cattle could be seen grazing near the village, and in other places on the floodplain we sometimes saw herds of up to a hundred head. The dung

*The Avocet forages in shallow water, sweeping its bill from side to side over the surface of the water or along the muddy bottom. The floodplain was the only place on the Zambezi where we encountered this species.*

produced through their presence on the plain during the dry season probably represents a good source of nutrient, filling a niche occupied by the substantial game population that was there in the past. The droppings attract swarms of flies to the area but are also useful in that they constitute a source of fuel. The plain is virtually devoid of trees so the villagers depend almost exclusively on the dried dung to make fires. Nature's annual clean-up takes place when the flood forces the beasts onto higher ground, thus providing the grasses with an opportunity to regenerate.

Further south on the floodplain we met Seki, who had a very different approach to fishing, preferring to operate at night. I arranged to accompany him on one of his forays and at the appointed time approached his small riverside village. At the water's edge wind-swept ripples splashed gently against the sides of four or five haphazardly parked dug-out canoes. Young, athletic-looking men moved casually around the beach folding nets and baling water out of the boats, while their light-hearted banter carried clearly over the water.

All activity came to a halt as the sound of my outboard motor intruded upon the tranquility and I nosed the rubber craft up onto the sand. By the time I had disembarked I was surrounded by black faces, all staring at an inflatable dinghy for the first time. An imitation of how a foot pump is used to inflate the craft drew wise nods and exclamations of understanding, while the sharp hiss of air as I demonstrated a valve sent a child scuttling up the beach in fright.

Gradually the novelty wore off and the people drifted back to their various tasks. I spotted Seki kneeling on the sand threading a cord to join two nets together. He wore a pair of shorts which had probably once been navy blue and reached almost down to his knees, but were split half way up one seam. His faded and tattered grey denim shirt was held closed at the front by a couple of metal buttons. The shirt hung loosely over his trousers and a shiny black shoulder glistened through a rent in the material. He was absorbed in his task, his bowed head sporting a dirty white sailor's cap which was a little small for him and gave the impression of being stuck by Velcro to his bushy black curls. In sharp contrast to the shabbiness of the rest of his attire, an ivory bracelet gleamed around his left wrist.

He glanced up at my approach and said, 'Tonight you are going to see a different style of fishing.' He pointed to a bundle of reeds, strapped together and tied to his nets. 'That will pull the net through the water. It will be like an ox.' He obviously felt it was not the sort of thing a makuwa would understand and added patiently, '... you will see.'

The last rays of the sun painted the grass huts a rich golden yellow and thin wisps of smoke drifted into the evening air as food was prepared for the departing fishermen. The western sky glowed pink, providing a delicately beautiful backdrop to the tall *Phragmites* reeds that loomed behind the vil-

*Lagoons and backwaters on the floodplain usually provide good fishing. Lozi fishermen often establish seasonal villages on their shores to exploit the bounty.*

lage. The first of the rivermen set off on their all-night excursion. Two men to a canoe, standing upright at bow and stern, propelling themselves against the current with paddles longer than the height of a man. Seki was in no hurry and had his nets laid out next to his boat. A string of stones along the bottom of the net serve as sinkers, while along the top reeds constitute floats. Seki's crew, a 15-year-old who had never been to school and knew no English, folded the net in concertina fashion into the centre of the boat, stones towards one end and floats towards the other.

While I sat on the beach watching the procedure a tall, broad-shouldered fellow clad simply in an old pair of brown corduroy shorts approached and asked, 'Are you not afraid of the mosquitoes?' I explained that I had a track-suit and had applied copious quantities of repellent cream to my delicate white skin to defend myself against such evils. When I voiced my reservations about the adequacy of his protection he was a little taken aback and explained, 'Ah, but I am an African and I have skin something like that of an animal. Even if they bite me I cannot suffer.'

After the last trace of day had disappeared, Seki placed a low wooden stool in the centre of his canoe on top of the net and gesturing towards it, said to me, 'We go now.'

Perched precariously on my little throne I looked ahead at the back of the crewman, who was manning the bow position, and heard the splash of Seki's paddle behind me. We slipped out into the darkness of the Zambezi night. There was about five centimetres space on either side between myself and the sides of the canoe, and as I gripped the rims my fingers were splashed by the water of our bow wave. I found myself involuntarily bracing this way and then that and tightening my grip, while my posterior teetered no more than 10 centimetres above Zambezi level. The only uncertainty surrounding my fate as I saw it, was whether I would ignominiously topple off my perch and plunge alone into the river, or whether I would capsize the whole craft. The last thing I needed was Seki's comment, 'The first thing a fisherman has to do is learn to swim well.' Pursuing this cheery line of conversation I asked if he ever actually had the problem of his boat turning over. His reply was emphatic, 'Ah! Always!' I told myself that his English was not good and that he meant 'sometimes' or 'often', but not 'always!' My grip tightened.

Gradually our balance improved and we made our way steadily downstream, mostly hugging the bank but occasionally striking out across the stream, when the men would paddle furiously and I would concentrate on keeping my stool upright.

Seki explained that it is more fruitful to fish at night because the fish can't see the nets. The four-inch gauge we were using would ensure that all the fish caught would be of two varieties of small-mouthed bream. His fishing techniques and quarry vary during the year. The annual floods which inundate the plain cause him to spend four months of the year at his permanent

LEFT *A Yellowbilled Stork dries its wings after fishing in shallow water. Not convinced of its motives, its partner plays coy!*
ABOVE *The Zambezi's clearly defined main channel cuts through the floodplain. These sand cliffs provide good nesting sites for such birds as Carmine and Whitefronted Bee-eaters.*

village some kilometres east of the river. While there he sets nets on the flooded plain to catch bream. During this time he supplements his income by collecting mangos and cycling to Senanga to sell them for 10 ngwee each. In May, with the water beginning to drain into the main channel tigerfish become the main target. At low water, like now, he prefers the technique we would use tonight, alternating it sometimes with 'pulling', whereby two men walk through the water with a net herding fish into the shore, where they catch them.

After travelling downstream for more than an hour, word was given for the passenger to move to the front of the boat. Somehow the crewman and I managed to slip past each other without falling prey to gravity. We paddled out into midstream, where the reed 'oxen', tied to one end of the net, was jettisoned. Unknown to me, the other end of the net had been fastened to the base of my stool. For half an hour we moved along the bank, keeping pace with the float, and gradually feeding out the full length of the net. Ultimately we turned out again into the stream to rendezvous with the float

– the net trailing behind like a bag. My stool started inching backwards, I gripped harder on the sides of the boat and pressed my backside down. Still I wasn't holding my position, so I grabbed the stool with both hands, whereupon sounds of confusion prompted me to peer behind into the darkness. The crewman was tugging at a rope which was evidently attached to my little piece of furniture and gradually I was made to understand that I had to raise myself if work was to proceed!

Each fisherman took an end of the net and they hauled it in, the occasional glint of silver in the darkness and the sound of wet fish slapping the bottom of the boat confirming that their efforts had not been in vain. We proceeded to shore and a further half hour was spent extracting the contents from the net, untangling it and folding it back into the boat. The total haul was six bream – apparently a disappointing catch.

The procedure was repeated. Although there was no moon, the night was cloudless and the fine array of stars cast enough light to save the scene from total darkness. The sky and the still surface of the river seemed to form a single entity, broken only by the dark horizontal strip of reeds along the bank. The sound of jovial voices heralded the passage of two men, who could be seen silhouetted on top of the bank. In the friendly way of the river people, Seki called out to them and exchanged pleasantries. He then chuckled and commented, 'They have been for beer drinking,' and admitted it was a pastime he too favoured.

53

I questioned Seki on his way of life. He thoughtfully repeated my questions before answering. 'What schooling have I had? Well, I went to school for four years before I became a fisherman and I have been fishing now for 14 years. Of course I enjoy fishing – it is my work and it brings me money. Even if I can find a job, I don't want it – I can make money with fishing and there is no problem with relish.'

Speaking of his family, Seki claimed to have nine children. When I voiced my incredulity, as he couldn't have been more than 35 years old, he explained that, 'Four are from my wife, three from my girlfriend and the others from different 'partners'.'

Over the next few hours we carried out four casts, ending up with a total catch of 41 bream, which formed a steadily growing, wet, slippery pile around my feet. All the while we progressed slowly downstream, the men using their paddles with practiced expertise – paddling in the deeper water,

poling against the bottom in the shallows, and occasionally using them as levers to push away from the bank.

We encountered two fellows using a completely different fishing technique. They had a paraffin lamp burning in the bow of their boat, with one of the fishermen hunched over it ready to plunge his spear into any fish attracted to the light.

At 01h00 in the morning the moon peered over the horizon like a half-closed, bloodshot eye. The cold had long since penetrated my tracksuit and my joints were stiff from my cramped position.

'You want your bed now,' Seki stated.

I protested but had to admit relief when he turned towards home, not believing that a makuwa could manage a whole night on the water.

'Usually we remain until the sun comes, but it is difficult in the boat with three people.'

54

ABOVE *Bulozi fishermen tend to operate mostly with nets, a limited range of which are available from Mongu and Senanga. Representing a sizeable investment, such equipment warrants careful maintenance.*
ABOVE RIGHT *Some fishermen prefer to net from their dug-out canoes at night. The gauge of this net will ensure a haul of small-mouthed bream.*

Not for the first time I was struck by the equanimity of the African people. Seki and his partner were completely unperturbed by the fact that their night's fishing had been curtailed by a silly makuwa who had 'stowed away' on their boat. Likewise they never showed any emotion at the size of their catch any time they pulled in their nets. They appeared to have a calm acceptance of all things.

At 03h00 the nose of our canoe ground onto the beach in front of the village, where there were still figures moving about in the moonlight.

Although I could only have been a hindrance, Seki graciously tossed four of the night's catch into my boat as if in recognition of my contribution to the work. When he in turn indicated his need for a new pair of shorts, I had no hesitation in removing those I wore under my tracksuit and bequeathing them to my captain.

Out in the open water I gave 'Skimmer' full throttle and revelled in the exhilaration of hurtling into the African night. The wake glistened faintly in the light of the half moon, the distant river banks seemed motionless in the gloom and cool air rushed into my face. What a river! What a life!

We spent most of our days on the floodplain mapping the occurrence of the various habitat types along the main channel and recording bird distribution. Despite the human activity, we found this to be the most prolific birding area of any we encountered on the Upper or Middle Zambezi. Flocks of waterfowl, storks and pelicans, multitudes of herons, gulls and

terns constantly demanded our attention. Scrutiny of the fertile mud and sand banks invariably yielded jewels like the nest of an African Skimmer or an Avocet, while the busy little waders foraging along the water's edge warranted close study to reveal the occasional species which we hadn't seen before. The first light of dawn would herald the emergence of exquisitely coloured bee-eaters from sandy burrows. During the day they decorated the skies with darting, acrobatic flight before re-congregating in chattering excitement when the sun went down.

The African Fish Eagle is widely known in Africa for its regal air as it surveys its dominion from a lofty bough. Here, however, on this saucer-flat expanse completely devoid of any kind of perch, the king was reduced to the level of common birds and had to settle for a place on the grassy river bank. Nevertheless, his manner was unchanged, and none would dare question his authority.

The African Skimmer – a bird of powerful, buoyant flight – is remarkable for its feeding technique. As it flies low over the water it dips its elongated lower bill into the water, scything a V-pattern across the surface, and scoops up small fish. Its breeding is confined to sandbanks on larger African rivers, and we were gratified to find in this area a greater number of nests than had ever been recorded elsewhere. The birds were incubating during the time of our visit and by the time we left the plain the first chicks had hatched.

Considering the human presence we were concerned about the vulnerability of the nests. The fishermen we spoke to said the eggs were too small to warrant collecting, but we did deduce in one instance that eggs had been removed by children. We were also distressed on a number of occasions to find traps on the sandbanks designed specifically for African Skimmers.

In addition to studying birds we spent a lot of time photographing them. Jumbo was the specialist in this field of endeavour, but we evolved an effective team approach for getting close to our subjects. Jumbo secreted himself in the nose of the boat under some shade cloth, with his 600-millimetre Novoflex lens forming a bowsprit. I would mould myself against the outside of the dinghy on the side away from the birds and gradually inch the boat towards our quarry. Depending on the depth of the water I conducted the manoeuvres by inching along the river bed on either my feet, knees or rear end. I frequently came close to blowing our cover by leaping into the

---

*In addition to being skilled fishermen, the Lozi rear cattle. Herds brought onto the plain in the dry season are forced back to higher ground by the annual flood, giving the grasses an opportunity to regenerate.*

boat when passing pieces of Kariba weed impersonated piercing crocodile eyes. These sessions sometimes lasted up to four hours, after which our joints had usually seized, but more often than not we were rewarded with satisfying photo opportunities.

Near the southern tip of the floodplain the main channel runs right up against the eastern escarpment at Senanga, with the plain stretching away to the west. We spent a few days in the town clearing our movements with the authorities because this was a high-security zone with the proximity of hostilities in Namibia and Angola. We eventually received clearance but were warned not to go downstream because we were likely to experience problems with the military.

Just upstream of Senanga is a wide and long lagoon which is bigger than the main Zambezi. Unfamiliar boatmen can easily travel several kilometres up the lagoon before coming to a dead end, which gives the lagoon its name, 'Wayama' – the lake of disappointment. However, we were quite adept at river travel by now and confident of our navigational ability. When we set out I was navigator so I showed Jumbo how to avoid the lagoon and also explained to him how the topography of the river had changed quite substantially since our map had been printed some 20 years earlier. I was a little irked that my expositions received scant acknowledgement from my partner and were in fact greeted with some scepticism. Undaunted, I ignored his churlishness. Suddenly I felt distinctly uneasy – things up ahead just didn't look right. Raising my binoculars I studied the scene and my heart skipped a beat – the right-hand bank was crawling with armed soldiers! We retreated immediately, trying to hide ourselves in the overhanging trees. We had travelled 15 kilometres in the wrong direction – heading downstream! Although I rationalized to Jumbo that even Stanley hadn't found the source of the Nile at the first attempt, my explanation did little to restore my credibility.

By the time we had completed our study of Bulozi, conditions had changed quite significantly. We no longer had clear skies with spectacular sunrises and sunsets. Palls of smoke rose from ubiquitous fires as cattle herders burned off the long grass and reeds to give their beasts access to the young grasses beneath. The impact on visibility was such that in the morning the sun only became visible as a dull orb once it had cleared the horizon by about 10 degrees. The burning undoubtedly removes a significant amount of nutrient from the floodplain, but this is probably compensated for by wind-blown deposition from the more fertile parts of Zambia which lie to the east.

# CATARACTS AND CAPRIVI

## SENANGA TO KAZUNGULA

*Mike Coppinger*

AFTER OBTAINING THE necessary permission from the authorities, we made a second attempt – this time legitimate – to boat downstream from Senanga. The easy boating of the floodplain became a thing of the past as the river entered rocky country. Outcrops at various levels of submersion in places formed barriers across the full width of the river, forcing us on occasion to disembark and pull the boat.

Apart from an extension of the floodplain for some 25 kilometres downstream of Senanga, the southbound river constitutes a lifeline through harsh, dry country. The banks assume a composition reminiscent of that above the Kabompo confluence, but differences are evident. The *Phragmites* reeds are accompanied by some other varieties of emergent vegetation and, with the exception of the floodplain protrusion, there is no evidence of inundation zones. In the riparian fringe *Syzygium* begins to lose its monopoly and *Garcinea livingstonei* becomes a conspicuous competitor. A feature of the river are a number of large islands, notably Mbeta which is 17 kilometres long and reaches a width of four kilometres. We generally found that the narrower channels to the east of these islands offered the more pleasant conditions for boating.

The change in habitat by comparison with that provided by the floodplain is accompanied by a dramatic decline in bird life. The only noteworthy aspect in this regard was the presence of significant numbers of Rock Pratincoles. In the month of September the water level was falling and these birds were beginning to stake their claim to midstream rocks which they would use as breeding sites.

After a full day's travel from Senanga we had covered 85 kilometres and just before sunset found the river becoming very wide, shallow and faster flowing. We were approaching the Ngonye Falls and in fading light made camp on a convenient island. In our haste we failed to realize that we had chosen a spot right next to a hippo trail. As a result we were subjected to a barrage of bad hippo language and angry displays through the course of the evening and eventually crawled into our sleeping bags feeling duly chastened and decidedly uneasy.

Our camp site was on one of a number of reed-fringed, wooded islands which bisect the Zambezi as it fans out on its approach to the falls. The wide western arm becomes a maze of narrow swift-flowing channels. Between these troughs the water spreads a glossy veneer over rock slabs and pebbles. Ultimately, along the craggy 1500-metre-wide lip of the falls the channels burst into a profusion of spectacular tumbling veils.

The narrower, papyrus-flanked eastern arm is initially deeper, until a rock barrier reduces the Zambezi to the undignified depth of a few centimetres. Two kilometres further on the character of this channel is changed dramatically. Funneled between the palm-dominated greenery of an island and bare mainland rock, a white torrent of foaming water is shredded by jagged stone as it plummets over the 10-metre fall.

Below the falls the flow of all these scattered cascades is marshalled by unyielding rock walls into a narrow, swift-flowing, purposeful body of water sweeping downstream.

The village of Sioma on the west bank of the falls partly owes its exis-

LEFT *Frederick Arnot once commented that the Sioma (Ngonye) Falls would be famous if the Victoria Falls didn't occur just 300 kilometres downstream. A proliferation of separate, enchanting cascades span a 1,5-kilometre-wide front.*
ABOVE *Baobab trees are common in hot dry woodland adjoining the Zambezi at lower altitudes.*

59

tence to the fact that the waterfall presents an obstacle to river traffic. Around the turn of the century access to Barotseland was gained by wooden barges which were paddled up the Zambezi from Livingstone. King Lewanika had men stationed at Sioma to portage the craft around the unnavigable cataracts.

During Lewanika's reign a number of independent, eccentric traders and adventurers followed the river into these remote lands. One of them, Arthur Harrington, lived virtually his whole life in Barotseland. Although trading was his livelihood – and to this day the Harrington store operates in Senanga – he also achieved renown as a fine boat builder. Harrington was a wild man, but was not regarded as unpleasant or vicious. In Livingstone he used to go to the cinema and invariably ended up shooting the villain on the screen. Equally trigger-happy back home at Senanga he often sat on his verandah and shot the calabashes off the heads of women carrying water up from the river!

In 1946, at the age of 73, Harrington visited England for the first time since his departure in 1897. Ted Spencer flew him over in a small charter plane after making special travel arrangements because Harrington refused to comply with the formality of getting a passport. Spencer had himself achieved the distinction of once flying up the Zambezi gorges and under the Victoria Falls Bridge. Upon arrival in London, Harrington stayed at the Savoy and, unmoved by the sophistication surrounding him, nightly performed native dances in front of the orchestra – much to the delight of the patrons! Harrington was a well-liked figure on the Upper Zambezi and when he died in Senanga at the age of 87, hundreds of Africans turned up to assist at his funeral. In fact the Barotse traders were generally respected by the Africans of the day. Lewanika ordered that all these residents of Barotseland be referred to as 'Morena' (chief).

'Trapper' Chipman, who originally came to Rhodesia to collect butterflies, walked up to Barotseland and never returned to civilization. He lived entirely off the bush, making his own footwear and fashioning clothes from animal skins, and was never known to procure supplies from Livingstone. He was acknowledged as a superb hunter with no sense of fear, but finally met his end at the horns of a buffalo. He had rescued his son from an attack by the animal but was himself fatally gored and subsequently buried at Sioma. By the time of his death he was an old man with only one tooth left but, typical of his resilient nature, he had still been able to chew biltong!

The solitary existence pursued by these pioneers inevitably affected their behaviour, as is evidenced by a story told of 'Trader' Brough. Sitting on his verandah one evening he saw a line of porters approaching, accompanied by a white man riding on a donkey. Brough had not seen an European for

*The Chobe River waters one of Africa's great wilderness areas. Lying to the south of the Caprivi Strip, Botswana's Chobe National Park provides sanctuary for a magnificent diversity of wildlife. The tourist industry supported by the park is a testimony to the economic value of such areas.*

many months and became excited – telling his servant to kill chickens, prepare a special meal and put out drinks. By the time the caravan arrived Brough found that he could not, without some mental preparation, face another white man and disappeared into his bedroom. The servant ensured that the visitor had drinks and dinner – but he ate alone. Only the next morning did his host gather the nerve to come out and talk!

A character who made his mark on the territory at an earlier time was Silva Antonio Francisco Porto. He was a Portuguese who travelled widely in Barotseland between 1849 and 1889 trading in goods and slaves. In 1890 Porto's village, in nearby Angola, was attacked during a local uprising. He was deeply insulted that this could happen to him after having been established in the area for so long. Such was his hurt that he wrapped himself in the Portuguese flag, lay down on a litter of 13 kegs of gunpowder and blew himself through the roof of his house. He fell to earth some distance away and died the following morning of shock.

Today a Catholic mission at Sioma makes positive contributions to many aspects of community life. When we returned to the area by road we were very hospitably received by the missionaries. Although our vehicle was not totally reliable, we could generally depend on her to misbehave only when help was at hand, almost in recognition of the fact that to count on her owners for meaningful help was hopeless! So it was conveniently in Sioma that she suffered a relapse and one of the brothers kindly spent the better part of a night solving our mechanical problems.

Interesting discussions with the missionaries underlined to us some of the realities of the southern African situation. The cross on the church hung limply from the roof because they had tired of replacing it after regular low-level flights by an intruding South African reconnaissance jet repeatedly blew it over. It was a reminder of the continuing hostilities in nearby Angola and Namibia which did from time to time boil over to engulf the Zambian people.

We also heard tales of high-technology, high-expenditure aid projects which had failed dismally. These stories reinforced our observations that the type of aid most likely to succeed was that which matched the sophistication of the local people. We had witnessed positive progress made by endeavours to promote bee-keeping, ox-cart manufacture and pottery production. These schemes were orientated around the local culture and resources, therefore they had a realistic chance of being adopted by the people and incorporated into their way of life.

In temperatures reaching 40°C we drove south along the river to Sesheke, where the Zambezi swings eastwards to form the border between Zambia and Namibia's Caprivi Strip. In the evening the lights of Katima Mulilo twinkled on the opposite bank. We knew the 'enemy' town well, having spent a couple of months there a year earlier, but with the absurdities that accompanied the regional hostilities we were not keen to display any signs of recognition.

A rough translation of the name 'Katima Mulilo' is 'to put out the fire'.

OPPOSITE *Endemic to swampy habitat is the Copperytailed Coucal, which does not occur south of the Okavango and Caprivi swamps. Of shy and secretive disposition, it is generally only seen when sunning itself.*
ABOVE *The merging of the Zambezi and Chobe rivers forms the Caprivi swamps – one of southern Africa's largest and remotest wetlands.*

There are two versions of the origin of the name. One is that canoe travellers paddling upstream would always carry fire embers in the canoe. From Mambova Rapids the water is smooth, but the rough waters at Katima could splash in and quench the coals. The second version is that travellers can wade across the rapids at Katima, where the swift-running water is no more than crotch deep. The long wade is enough to douse any fires of passion the traveller may have had!

At the time of our visit to Caprivi, in mid-1986, the South African Defence Force maintained a strong presence in the territory. A navy barge plied the river between Katima and Mpalela Island at the eastern tip of the strip, providing a ferry service for the local people. We were fortunate enough to be able to make the passage.

It was a full day's voyage to the island, so we wrapped ourselves up against the dawn chill and gingerly guided our truck and trailer onto the vessel. Our vehicles dominated the boat – the remaining space being crammed with Caprivi village folk. Surrounded by trading goods and personal belongings they chattered excitedly, their voices competing with the throb of the diesel engines.

Travelling downstream we soon saw the fringing forest recede, to be replaced by reedbeds stretching to the horizon. We were traversing the northern perimeter of a large swamp formed by merging Zambezi and Chobe floodplains (*see* map). The inhabitants of the swamp lead a migratory life governed by the rise and fall of the water level. The flood was near its peak in May, and had inundated many dry-season dwellings. Remaining fishing villages perched precariously on any ground elevations which provided a solid platform in this watery world.

In areas where sandbanks were still exposed the bird life was dramatic. Particularly spectacular were flocks of several thousand Redwinged Pratincoles periodically spiralling up from the sand. From a distance their towering columns resembled vast swarms of bees.

Mpalela Island lies in the fork of the Zambezi-Chobe confluence. This is a transitional zone where the river passes from the exceptionally flat, sandy terrain of the Caprivi into an area that is cloaked by ancient lava flows. The hills of Chobe lying to the south are conspicuous after the level horizons afforded by the swampland. Mpalela itself is for the most part slightly more elevated than the rest of Caprivi, therefore constituting a refuge from the flood waters and attracting a higher population than most parts of the region. After disembarking at Mpalela we made camp on the banks of a small stream that bisected the island. It was a wild, luxuriant setting with clear bubbling waters bordered by lush evergreen trees. Sound effects were provided by the evocative call of a stately African Fish Eagle, backed up by the baritone grunts of a local herd of hippos.

Exploration of the island revealed a significant presence of two tree species not encountered on the upper reaches of the Zambezi but characteristic of hot, low-lying parts of tropical southern Africa, namely the Mopane (*Colophospermum mopane*) and Baobab (*Adansonia digitata*). The baobab is a fascinating tree with a huge trunk, measuring about 28 metres in circumference in large specimens, topped by short stubby branches. The unusual appearance has led some African tribes to believe that God planted the trees

ABOVE *The hills of the Chobe overlook the panorama of the Caprivi swamps. Herds of big game are often scattered across the tapestry of water and reed.*
OPPOSITE *Elephant are a dominating presence in the Chobe National Park.*

upside down. We saw one impressive example in the local chief's village. This tree had a hollow trunk accessible via two entrances and in the past was used as a committee room for important meetings. Occupation of the chamber has now been taken over by a family of Barn Owls. A more common use of the tree is provided by its edible fruit, which contains appreciable quantities of tartaric acid and potassium bitartrate. We were amused to see a group of small barefoot children walking to school carrying baobab pods as their 'lunch boxes'.

From vantage points on the island we could see three other countries. The northern bank of the Zambezi is Zambian territory, while to the south of the Chobe and just touching the Zambezi at the confluence is the Republic of Botswana. Adjacent to Botswana and immediately downstream of the confluence lies Zimbabwean territory.

The Chobe is a tributary which is an intriguing and important river in its own right. It begins life as the Cuando which, like the Okavango and

Lunguevungu, rises in the bountiful highlands of Angola. Over the 800-kilometre passage from source to its rendezvous with the Zambezi at Kazungula the river undergoes several name changes. As the Cuando it traverses Angolan territory. Cutting through the Caprivi Strip it is known as the Kwando and later the Mashi. The river then spills into the Linyanti swamps and adopts that name when it emerges to flow east into Lake Liambezi. The final identity of Chobe is attained when it completes its course from the lake to the Zambezi confluence.

The remarkably flat topography of the region surrounding the Linyanti and Chobe, coupled with the number of sizeable rivers in the vicinity, have conjured up a fascinating hydrological scenario. One unusual feature is that the direction of the Chobe's flow is sometimes reversed. This happens when the Zambezi flood level is higher than the level of the Chobe and the waters of the main river then push back up the channel of the tributary. Also, when the Zambezi is high, its flood overflow can reach Liambezi via the Bukalo mulapo (channel).

The Chobe gives rise to another interesting phenomenon in that it links the Zambezi and Okavango River systems. On the one hand the Okavango can drain into the Linyanti via the Selinda Spillway, while the Linyanti swamps feed the Savuti channel.

In addition to introducing two new countries to the Zambezi, we found that the Chobe also brought with it the presence of vast numbers of Africa's big game. The dominant life forms on the upper river thus far had been people, birds and fish. We were to find that for the next 800 kilometres downstream wildlife would become a prominent feature, particularly on the southern bank.

Whereas we had become accustomed to navigating our way around hippos a new hazard was encountered when boating up the Chobe – swimming elephants. These magnificent giants come down to the waterfront in large numbers and sometimes cross over to partake of the alluring greenery of the Caprivi swamps. They give every indication of enjoying the swim – at times completely submerging themselves, with just the tips of their trunks protruding above the water like snorkels.

The 'jumbos' have a profound impact on Chobe's environment. Unlike the Zimbabweans, the Botswanan authorities have pursued a policy of not culling the elephant population. This heavy concentration of pachyderms has resulted in a landscape littered with broken trees, creating an impression, particularly in the dry season, of devastation. In the course of feeding the powerful beasts push over trees to get at foliage or roots, and also have a tendency to strip the bark with their tusks. The baobab does not escape the elephants' attentions, but one of the tree's exceptional qualities is its ability to survive ring-barking. Nonetheless the animals have a liking for the plant's fibrous pulp and do on occasion demolish and consume an entire specimen.

The abundance of animal life in Botswana's Chobe National Park is contrasted by the comparative scarcity in Caprivi. As recently as the mid-1970s the eastern Caprivi supported a healthy wildlife population particularly

notable for tens of thousands of lechwe, a water-loving antelope species. The game has now been decimated by poaching, with fewer than 5 000 lechwe remaining in 1986, virtually all in the vicinity of Nkasa and Lupala islands in the Linyanti swamps. At the time of our visit this swamp region was uninhabited even though it did not enjoy any legislative protection. The Linyanti owes the maintenance of its relatively pristine condition to a long-time custodian of African wilderness – the tsetse fly. Nkasa and Lupala were formerly inhabited by members of the Mafwe tribe, but they were forced to withdraw to the Sangwali district in the 1960s to escape the ravages of trypanosomiasis, a fatal disease transmitted by the tsetse.

We had the marvellous opportunity to visit Nkasa with Neil Macdonald, a Namibian Nature Conservation official, and his tracker, Boniface. At the time of our visit water levels had been low for several years, with the result that there were extensive dry areas, and the water flow was confined to some well-defined streams. Alongside one of these channels we established a rudimentary camp from where Neil and Boniface commenced their patrols. On their first outing Boniface detected poachers' spoor, which led them to a camp which was extremely well concealed in a belt of trees bordering a reed-filled swamp. The intrepid rangers stormed the camp causing

eight surprised poachers to scatter in disarray. One of their number was brought to earth and apprehended by Neil. They abandoned several axes, rifles and spears as well as a considerable amount of meat which was hanging out to dry. By examining the carcasses we established that their bag had consisted of five lechwe, two hippo and one warthog. To find one of the hippo carcasses we had to follow the poachers' trail out into the swamp for an hour – often wading through icy, waist deep water. The apprehension caused us by the severe restriction of our vision by the four-metre-high papyrus reeds was heightened by the observation of fresh lion spoor following the same trail! The scene of the crime revealed the pitiful spectacle of the hippo's head lying in a pool of water with the pelvis and the bones of one leg lying nearby. To our relief, the lion had already eaten and departed.

Neil followed up the incident by going into Sangwali village, where he and Boniface were subjected to very menacing threats and abuse, but succeeded in arresting five of the remaining gang members. While we remained at Nkasa, Neil transported his captives back to Katima Mulilo. They would be tried and if found guilty faced a maximum sentence of a R50 fine per poached animal. Their weapons would not necessarily be confiscated. The woefully outdated statute under which such cases were tried was promulgated in 1927. The meat from one hippo could be sold for R400 so it made good business sense for a poacher to run the relatively small risk of capture.

Despite the apparent futility of his task, Neil returned to Nkasa where he made another arrest of five men. He also discovered a number of recently abandoned camps. We felt the hostility of the local population when we finally left the area after two weeks. Driving through a village near Sangwali we made the error of getting stuck in deep sand. With a bit of manpower we could have shoved the vehicle out of trouble fairly easily but the villagers, many of whom were drunk, refused to give any assistance. We spent the better part of the day providing local entertainment by digging and pushing to extricate ourselves.

---

LEFT *Barred Owl chicks peep out into the night from the security of their nest in a tree at Kazungula.*

OPPOSITE *Lesser bushbabies are nocturnal and arboreal, renowned for their leaping abilities. The animal's distribution range extends along most of the Zambezi's length. Its habitat preference is acacia or mopane woodland, but it can also be found in various mixed vegetation types.*

There can be no doubt that the poaching is having a very detrimental effect on the ecology of the region. It is equally clear that the activity is an important part of the local economy. What is not so clear is whether the current sorry state of Caprivi's wildlife is the result of this kind of local poaching or has been inflicted by more sophisticated outside exploitation. Either way, the devastation of natural resources is making life increasingly difficult for the local people. Unless dramatic steps are taken to control and sustain utilisation of these resources the village folk face a bleak future.

Caprivi's population of approximately 45 000 has descended from the tribes of Angola and Barotseland. There are two dominant groups, the Mafwe who essentially occupy the western portion of the territory, and the Masubia to the east of the Katima-Ngoma land bridge. The majority of the people are engaged in subsistence fishing and agriculture.

An important fishing ground is Lake Liambezi. The lake has been known to dry up in the past and it did so again in 1986, thus curtailing the food supply. It is quite possible that the process was accelerated by the fact that the reduced hippo population is no longer effective in keeping open the channels which feed the lake from the Linyanti swamps. It also illustrates how uncontrolled exploitation of one element of the environment can have an unexpected negative effect.

Caprivi does not have any real tourist infrastructure but an interesting development in 1986 was the declaration of a Natural Biotic Area in the eastern floodplain. Within this area the current population will remain and pursue their traditional way of life, but no commercial development or large influx of people will be permitted. A concession will be granted to a commercial concern to conduct photographic and fishing safaris in the area. A percentage of the revenue thus generated will be paid to the local population. If this strategy can be successfully implemented the environment will represent a source of revenue for the people and they will therefore have a tangible motive for preserving it.

A fresh chapter in Caprivi's history was opened with Namibia's attainment of independence in 1990. This development is bound to have far-reaching implications. The South African Defence Force and civil service presence was the backbone of the territory's infant economy. Apart from the economic consequences of their departure, there will obviously be a significant impact on all aspects of local government. We pray that in this new era Caprivi's unique environment will receive the careful management it so desperately requires.

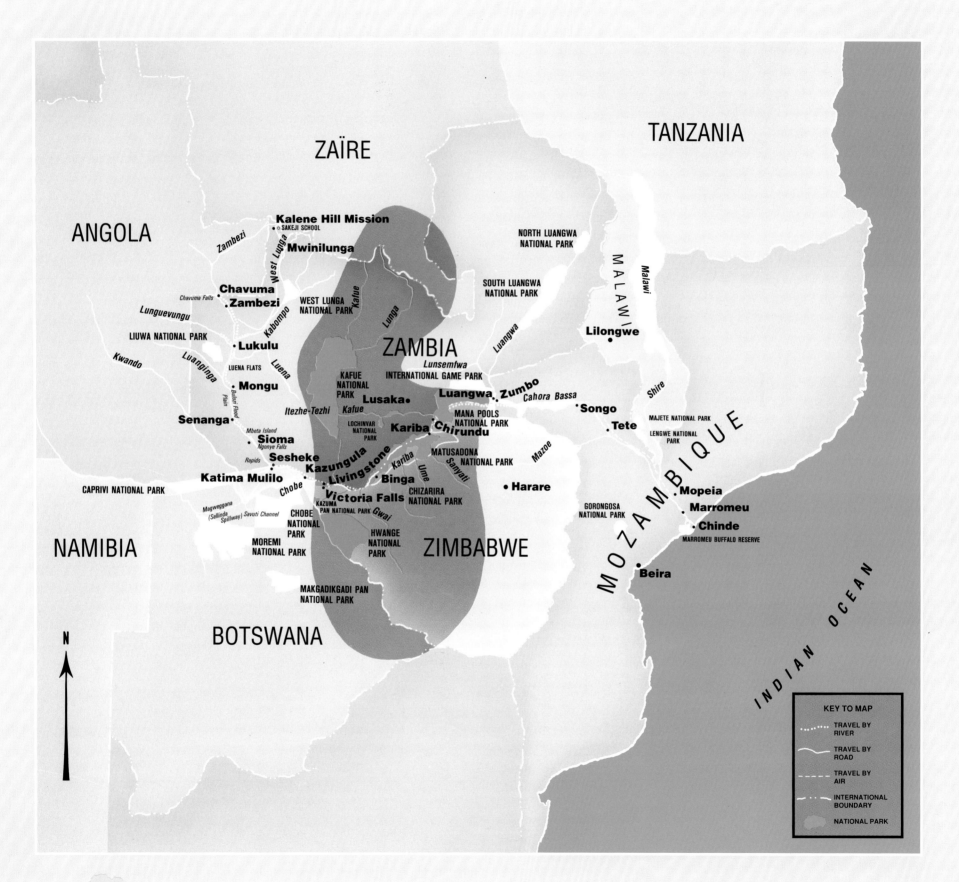

ZAÏRE

TANZANIA

ANGOLA

Kalene Hill Mission
○ SAKEJI SCHOOL

NORTH LUANGWA
NATIONAL PARK

*Zambezi*
*West Lunga*

Mwinilunga

SOUTH LUANGWA
NATIONAL PARK

Chavuma
*Chavuma Falls*
Zambezi

WEST LUNGA
NATIONAL PARK

*Kafue*

*Lunga*

M
A
L
A
W
I

*Malawi*

*Lunguevungu*

LIUWA NATIONAL PARK

*Kabompo*

ZAMBIA

*Luangwa*

Lilongwe

*Luena FLATS*

Lukulu

*Lunsemfwa*
INTERNATIONAL GAME PARK

*Kwando*

*Luanginga*

*Luena*

Mongu

KAFUE
NATIONAL
PARK

Luangwa • Zumbo

*Cahora Bassa*

*Shire*

Lusaka•

Songo

Senanga •

*Itezhe-Tezhi*

*Kafue*

MANA POOLS
NATIONAL PARK

Tete

MAJETE NATIONAL PARK

*Mbeta Island*

Sioma

LOCHINVAR
NATIONAL
PARK

Kariba •

Chirundu

LENGWE NATIONAL
PARK

*Ngonye Falls*

Sesheke

*Rapids*

Kazungula

*Kariba*

MATUSADONA
NATIONAL PARK

*Mazoe*

M
O
Z
A
M
B
I
Q
U
E

*Bulozi Flood Plain*

Katima Mulilo

*Chobe*

Livingstone

Binga

*Ume*

*Sanyati*

Victoria Falls

CHIZARIRA
NATIONAL PARK

• Harare

Mopeia

CAPRIVI NATIONAL PARK

*Magweggana
(Sellinda
Spillway)  Savuti Channel*

KAZUMA
PAN NATIONAL PARK

*Gwai*

Marromeu

CHOBE
NATIONAL
PARK

HWANGE
NATIONAL
PARK

ZIMBABWE

GORONGOSA
NATIONAL PARK

Chinde

NAMIBIA

MOREMI
NATIONAL PARK

MARROMEU BUFFALO RESERVE

MAKGADIKGADI PAN
NATIONAL PARK

Beira

I
N
D
I
A
N

O
C
E
A
N

N

BOTSWANA

KEY TO MAP

········ TRAVEL BY
RIVER

⌒⌒⌒ TRAVEL BY
ROAD

--- TRAVEL BY
AIR

-··-··- INTERNATIONAL
BOUNDARY

◖ NATIONAL PARK

# THE MIDDLE RIVER

*Tranquillity.*

# THUNDERING SMOKE

## KAZUNGULA TO VICTORIA FALLS

*Jumbo Williams*

JUST DOWNSTREAM OF THE Chobe-Zambezi confluence, the boundaries of Namibia, Botswana, Zambia and Zimbabwe merge at the small dishevelled settlement of Kazungula. Here, a ferry plies across the Zambezi, providing a valuable means of access and trade between the neighbouring nations. On account of its location, Kazungula has historically often assumed a role of some importance. Even in centuries past, long before the European imposition of international borders, the region served as a pivotal area of transition between cultures. It was here that Sebitwane crossed the Zambezi and led his marauding Suthu warriors northwards to conquer Barotseland. David Livingstone knew Sebitwane (the chief died in his arms) and it was his son Sekeletu who directed the pioneering missionary eastwards from Kazungula to the great waterfall that Livingstone was to name after his sovereign queen.

Later, in August 1882, F.S. Arnot passed through the same district, making his way upstream to establish Plymouth Brethren ministries. He noted of the river: 'Everything is the perfection of beauty and symmetry, only man is vile.'

This opinion seemed validated in recent years when the zone around Kazungula became enmeshed in Zimbabwe's civil war. The ferry was incapacitated by military action and trans-Zambezi traffic virtually ceased.

Now the ferry is fully operational, and from our Zimbabwean camp we could hear its engines clanking daily against the unremitting current. It was mid-November and the first rains of the wet season were drumming exuberantly against our tent's canvas roof. When the storm abated we celebrated with Mike's famous boerewors, eggs and potato hash, and watched ascending spirals of flying ants escape from the moist earth. European Swifts, those debonair migratory sun-worshippers, flitted among them, gulping down the airborne cuisine. A multitude of chongololos (millipedes) appeared and covered the campground, benignly nosing their way into utensils, sleeping bags and shoes.

Although Mpalela's rocky outcrops herald a transformation in the river's surroundings, at Kazungula the Zambezi reverts for a while to the themes of Caprivi. It eases along on sand, gently limited within flat banks of Waterberry, *Hyphaene* palms and papyrus. The locality is ornithologically important to Zimbabwe, for its limited floodplain hosts a large variety of wetland birds. In addition, the riparian woodland supports a breeding colony of Whitebacked Vulture, yet another species of dwindling numbers.

Eleven kilometres downstream of our Kazungula camp, the Zambezi abruptly and irrevocably alters its character. First the river surges down the frothy Katambora rapids and then for the next 50 kilometres is confused and fragmented by basalt bedrock into a maze of shallow channels. The waterway becomes dotted with islands. Many are formed entirely by low-lying rock. However, some of the larger islands support luxuriant riparian woodland and the ubiquitous *Phragmites* reed fringes.

Our investigations centred principally on the Rock Pratincole, a petite, dapper grey bird with distinctive white facial markings and a bright red gape. The Rock Pratincole is an endemic intra-African migrant and frequents the larger sub-Saharan rivers. The species has evolved a breeding

LEFT *'The countless jets and streams assume all colours and all forms; some are bright and gleaming, some dark and sombre; but as they plunge impetuously into the depth below they make up a spectacle that cannot fail to excite a sensation of mingled astonishment and delight.'* (E. Holub, 1881.)
ABOVE *Fireballs (*Haemanthus *sp.) glow within the rain forest.*

pattern that exploits nesting sites that are virtually ignored by other species. Such specialized behaviour offers the advantage of decreased competition but incorporates an inherent vulnerability, should the preferred habitat change radically.

Rock Pratincole arrive at the Zambezi during the period June to August. No-one knows whence they come or whither they depart after breeding. Territories are staked out on small rocky islands and pair-bonds cemented through a variety of courtship rituals. Usually two or three eggs are laid on bare stone; no effort is made to construct a nest. Only those rocks which are well isolated by fast-flowing water are chosen for a breeding site, and consequently predation by land animals is virtually excluded. In addition, the eggs are superbly camouflaged. They are mottled grey and overlain with a streaky lattice of black lines so that they blend perfectly into the background of basalt rocks.

In fact, the biggest threat to egg viability must be high temperatures. In the desiccating Zambezi heat of August to October, we often recorded surface rock temperatures that exceeded the scale of our 50 °C thermometer. Without continual shading by the parents, the embryos would inevitably succumb. Nest attendance exposes the adults to considerable heat load and their little bodies shake from vigorous panting. Both parents incubate and they frequently relieve each other from nest duty so as to allow the sitting bird a chance to cool down and drink. It was while watching the off-duty parent at the river's edge that we observed some unexpected behaviour. The bird stood in the shallows and rapidly dipped its underparts into the water. The gesture was so unlike their normal dainty drinking pose that on the first occasion I assumed the individual had lost its footing, collapsed in the water, and then immediately recovered. This 'drop-sitting' (as we termed it) was noted repeatedly and occurred more often during hot days.

In fact the birds did not engage in the activity at all when the sky was overcast. This is a form of 'belly wetting', an activity described in several bird families, including Glareolidae – of which the Rock Pratincole is a member. The presumed purpose in this case is to wet the brood feathers that embrace the eggs, so that during incubation the eggs become coated with a sheen of water which, by the latent heat of evaporation, cools the eggs. This had not been described with regard to the Rock Pratincole and we subsequently published a paper on our findings.

The young are well camouflaged, to the point of invisibility. They escape the sun by retreating under rock overhangs and into crevices. The

LEFT *African Fish Eagles are early risers and call at the first hint of dawn. This sets off a cascade of echoing calls as neighbouring pairs reply.*
RIGHT *Upstream of the Victoria Falls the Zambezi is broad, shallow and strewn with scattered outcrops of basalt rock.*
OVERLEAF *'The whole body of water rolls clear over, quite unbroken; but, after a descent of ten or more feet, the entire mass suddenly becomes like a huge sheet of driven snow.'* (D. and C. Livingstone, 1865.)

Rock Pratincole has thus capitalized on exposed midstream rocks as a relatively safe haven from predation and has evolved competent measures for dealing with heat stress.

However, one major factor governing their reproductive success remains beyond their control. The Zambezi, like most African rivers, is highly seasonal and the islands used for nesting are deeply submerged during the months of flooding. It is imperative that the birds commence breeding before the river rises too high. Yet the rainy season brings not only floods, but also an abundance of flying insects – the major constituent of a Rock Pratincole family's diet. It has been suggested that the visual stimulus of midstream rocks triggers the breeding cycle, allowing the species (in an average season) sufficient time for their young to be flying before the host rocks disappear. We think this theory could well be correct. Rock Pratincoles breeding in the steep, narrow gorges below the Victoria Falls were a full month ahead in schedule when compared to those pairs nesting further upstream, where the river is broad and shallow. Any change in water volume results in a far greater variation in river level in the constricted gorges than it does above the Falls. Thus the trigger to breed there should occur earlier, and our observations support the hypothesis.

Methodically searching for Rock Pratincole eggs proved quite a demanding exercise. Indeed, we found manouevring the inflatable among the surging, often shallow rapids was our trickiest boat work to date. Even with canoeist Mike's white water expertise we still incurred punctures and damaged several propellers. Nonetheless, the studies were hardly an arduous task for us. The setting was enchanting; sunbleached heavens, prancing water and magenta dragonflies.

Game frequented the Zimbabwean shore and we soon noticed that waterbuck males were in rut. At Katambora one came crashing through the thorn scrub and plunged into the Zambezi. His rival followed in close pursuit and waded out chest deep to glare his displeasure at the vanquished, who by now was showing only his nose and eyes above water. Over the next ten minutes the aggressor gradually permitted his adversary to cautiously regain dry land. We were fascinated, but unfortunately they then both caught whiff of our scent and retreated from view.

Waterbuck often descended the river's embankment beside our Sansimba camp and moved onto a small flat pasture that was accommodated by an outward sweep of the Zambezi. Four females were grazing there one afternoon when we spied a lioness walking parallel to the embankment but far back enough from the edge so as to be out of the waterbuck's sight. The herbivores smelt her, for they bunched nervously together but appeared

LEFT *Inquisitive vervet monkeys are often seen in the rain forest canopy, peering down on the camera-toting primates below.*
OPPOSITE *The Trumpeter Hornbill frequents the rain forest. Its voice is thus described: 'Very loud braying, laughing, trumpeting, squealing and wailing.' Call it what you like, the sound is unmistakable!*

uncertain just where the danger lay. It seemed a perfect ambush situation, as the lioness was well positioned to cut off the antelope's only line of escape. What is more, they had a four-metre bank to climb. However, the cat was either a poor tactician or not hungry, for she ambled into direct view and descended onto the plain with a half-hearted charge. Thus committed in the open, the lioness gave the waterbuck an excellent opportunity to exit in safety. This they duly took and we missed some gory campsite action.

Beyond Kandahar Island the Zambezi coalesces into a single broad channel and glides sublimely towards its precipitous destiny. In those few kilometres before the Victoria Falls, the river accommodates several large islands, named – to our parochial dismay – after 19th century English royalty. These islands are prolifically crowned by tropical forest. Elephants wade out to them in full view of appreciative tourists to browse in undisturbed luxury. We found the islands concealed other prizes, for example Pel's Fishing Owl, Collared Palm Thrush and Whitebacked Night Heron. Boating in the preliminary cascades immediately above the Victoria Falls also added zest to the enterprise.

John Coppinger (Mike's brother) and his wife Carol joined us for a week's vacation away from their safari business. We all piled into 'Skimmer' and ventured out to the islands in search of an elusive waterbird, the African Finfoot. Our quarry, once sighted, swam for the refuge of fringe vegetation. John, Mike and Carol were up front while I sat further back and handled the motor. We glided under the overhanging trees, John brushing away impeding low-lying branches. Unfortunately he never saw the nest until it was too late.

'Bees!' yelled John.

The insects swarmed out to challenge us. Mike leapt to the stern and slammed the engine into reverse. His concentration was, however, painfully diverted by the rapid-fire acquisition of several stings, so that the propeller ran afoul of reeds and the machine stalled. By now the front occupants had transformed themselves into human windmills, arms flailing disjointedly in every direction. The staccato slapping of hands against flesh served as percussion accompaniment to their woeful and frustrated curses. I disentangled the propeller, fired the motor, swung the boat around and headed in reckless flight for open water. The bees followed with a vengeance. John's face and head were coated in blood and his vigorous movements had spattered flecks of red all around the boat. 'Good grief!' I thought, 'What have these killer bees done?'

At last we outdistanced our tormentors, the windmills wound down and we regrouped. John and Carol had borne the brunt of the onslaught, Mike received half a dozen stings and I was unscathed. But what of the blood that still streamed down our guest's face? In his initial inspired defence, John's whirlwind activity had exceeded his body's mechanisms of fine co-ordination, so that he had delivered onto his own nose a full clenched bunch of fives. We stared incredulously at John's blood-smeared sheepish grin, a giggle surfaced, then another, until some ten minutes later Mike's irrepressible

laughter could still be heard mingling downstream with the gurgling river.

It was on the 16th November 1855 that David Livingstone first gazed, from the island that now bears his name, into the thundering chasm of the Victoria Falls. His descriptions of the experience initiated a stream of tourists which continues unabated to this day. This is Mosi oa Tunya, The Smoke That Thunders – greatest waterfall of them all.

The flat terrain surrounding the Victoria Falls gives the tourist little reason for expectation and only the ascending spray-clouds allude to the spectacular ravines ahead. Insight into the formation of this area of topographical contradictions is useful as it provides one with a greater appreciation of the Falls themselves.

It is thought that in the past the Upper Zambezi shared tributaries with the Zaïre River complex and at one stage flowed into the Limpopo system. A southern upward warp of the earth's crust caused pooling in the Makarikari-Chobe region and an eastward diversion of the Upper Zambezi. This facilitated its capture by the old Middle Zambezi headwaters - the present Matetsi River. The initial Victoria Falls were situated where the Upper Zambezi waters poured down the 250-metre western flank of the Matetsi Valley. With time, the Falls migrated upstream as powerful erosive forces carved out what is now the Batoka Gorge.

The feature that makes the Falls unique among the great waterfalls of the world is the zigzag shape and steepness of its gorges. The region was covered in volcanic basalt during the Jurassic period and as the lava cooled, cracks were formed in the hard rock. Those running east-west were emphasized by movements of the earth's crust and became filled with soft material. Near Livingstone the Zambezi turns south. This allowed erosion of the softer deposits within the cracks and the creation of a broad-fronted waterfall. Gradual erosion of small joints that run north-south caused the river to be concentrated into a narrow fissure and the broad fall-line was abandoned. Once this happened it was only a question of time before the narrow gorge cut back into another transverse fracture zone of soft material. The gouging out of this soft zone again established a broad fall. This process has been repeated over many years and the zigzag gorges represent seven abandoned wide-based Victoria Falls. (G. Bond, 1975)

At the present time the Falls are 1 708 metres in width and have a maximum height of 103 metres. Since the bulk of the water which passes over the Falls is derived not from rainfall in the immediate vicinity, but from that in regions far upstream, there is an appreciable time lag between the season of peak rainfall and that of the highest flow of water over the Falls. Generally, the lowest level is in late November or early December, well after the start of the rainy season. During this period the mean flow is less than 20 000 cubic metres per minute and allows relatively mist-free panora-

*An aerial view of Victoria Falls from the Zimbabwean bank reveals the switchback gorges formed by ancient fall sites.*

LEFT *In the dry season the water flowing over the Eastern Cataract is shallow enough to allow one to wade out from the Zambian bank to the island from which David Livingstone first viewed Mosi oa Tunya.*
ABOVE *The petite Rock Pratincole can be seen on rock islands near the lip of the Falls. It may breed there, for we saw local children checking under ledges, presumably for chicks.*

mas. Then, as the wet season proceeds, the water level rises rapidly and peaks in March or April, averaging 550 000 cubic metres per minute. This is an increase of some 30 times from the dry-season volume. Spray is so dense that the drenched spectator cannot see much at all. Everything but the wall of water immediately ahead is swathed in a diffuse curtain of rising spray.

'It drips in torrents from every branch and leaf, rustles in the coarse grass, lies in pools on the ground and in a very few minutes soaks the sightseer to the skin.' (Lord Curson of Kedleston, 1923).

Like most tropical African rivers, the Zambezi has a distinct fringing vegetation of riparian woodland. The Rain Forest is an unusually extensive area of riverine growth and is made possible by the continuous spray from the Falls. These conditions are particularly favourable to small moisture-loving plants and a highly specialized flora has evolved that contains many endemics. Over 400 species have been identified and add yet another complexity to the intriguing Falls ecology. In truth, one needs to revisit the Falls frequently in order to savour all its facets and moods.

ABOVE *Construction of the bridge began in 1904. The gorge was crossed by firing a rocket attached to a string, which was used to haul across a rope and then a steel cable. A bosun's chair was put into operation and one could make the crossing in about ten minutes.*

OPPOSITE *When the river is low, a Zambian-based rafting company, Sobek, can row upstream from the Boiling Pot to the very base of the Victoria Falls. It is a unique experience and quite overwhelming.*

There are many wondrous aspects to the Zambezi, but if one were limited to visiting only one location on the river, we would heartily recommend the Victoria Falls. In the idiom of today's young, the Falls are 'awesome'. We retreated into the unpretentious library at Livingstone town and discovered a rich cache of old literature on the early exploration of the Falls. 'Awesome' appeared equally applicable in days gone by. It seemed that a common theme of the chronicles describing the Falls was the emotions evoked by the spectacle. Mosi oa Tunya engenders emotion; it is not a passive experience.

'It seemed to me as if my own identity were swallowed up in the surrounding glory, the voice of which rolled on forever, like the waves of eternity. ... No human being can describe the infinite; and what I saw was a part of infinity made visible and framed in beauty.' (E. Mohr, 1876).

'It is hell itself, a corner of which seems to open at your feet: a dark and terrible hell, from the middle of which you expect every moment to see some repulsive monster rising in anger.' (L. Decle, 1898).

'To my mind the Victoria Falls of the Zambezi are one of the most imposing phenomena of the world. ... Truly it is a scene in which a man may well become aware of his own insignificance!' (E. Holub, 1881).

We were similarly moved. For me the first impression was unmistakable: immense power, the raw energy unleashed when the entire Zambezi leaps wildly into a black two-kilometre-wide abyss. The image generated has many of the symbols encountered in mythology to signify overwhelming supernatural forces or godly powers. The scale is massive, the spectacle spellbinding and perpetually changing. The Falls hiss and roar as if possessed, they rumble and crash like thunder. Vast clouds spew and billow out from the seething cauldron of its dark impenetrable depths. The moving water creates a magnetism that sucks you closer, so that you recoil in horror to quench a subliminal sacrificial urge.

The Falls are life-giving and bountiful. They represent Mother Nature, the generous supporter of myriad and prolific life forms. Whether one applies a magnifying glass to detail the lichen-draped bark of the rain forest, or gazes from afar at rainbows arching over a cataract, the scene is breathtaking. Early, when dawn sulphur-tints wisps of rising spray and the grass is still bejewelled with condensation, bushbuck timidly venture out from forest shadows to feed. They nibble on the lush plants at the edge of the precipice and stand wraith-like amid the swirling patterns of mist and dappled sunlight. To my mind this image represented detailed perfection.

Mosi oa Tunya can also be a refuge to indulge in inner reflection, a place to reconsider life's goals, to contemplate the marvels of nature, man's deficient knowledge and the inadequacies within our souls.

The spectacle presented by the Falls is unimaginably beautiful, continually overloading the senses. There are endless moments of magic: lunar rainbows on a full moon's rise; soaking deluges of windblown spray; a cacophony of raucous hornbills; fire-red blossoms nestled secretly within tangled recesses of greenery.

Consequently the area abounds with tourists; camera-toting, giggling, sweating, marvelling, sombre, polite, brash, informed, lost and restless humanity. There is no other region on the Zambezi where people congregate in such numbers. Indeed tourism is a flourishing industry and the economic foundation for local inhabitants. So it should be, and Zambia and Zimbabwe can profit by sharing their wonderful heritage with the world. The impact on the environment has been, in our opinion, well managed. Paths are satisfactorily maintained and sightseers efficiently confined to them. Structures within the Park are aesthetically pleasing and unobtrusive. I have no doubt that escalating numbers of visitors will become the principal challenge for the guardians of Mosi oa Tunya. Such concerns are already paramount in popular wilderness areas like Yosemite and Yellowstone in the United States.

Apart from the personnel servicing the hotels and tourist trade, Victoria Falls has a collection of residents of altogether another genre. These are the safari operators and white-water guides. Sharing a common bond of an adventurous and outdoor lifestyle, this small group used to congregate for congenial company at the offices of a business concern called S.O.S. Our story centres around Jeremy, an entrepreneur in his early twenties and the hospitable proprietor of S.O.S.

Jeremy was a jovial, fast-talking man, obviously very comfortable in the convivial friendship of his hard-living patrons. However, youth has the disadvantage of inexperience and he was perhaps a little piqued when one particularly wild hunter roundly proclaimed Jeremy to be the ultimate wimp. Extrication from this despicable condition was offered at a price – he had to complete certain specified tasks. The first of these assignments (mundane, of course, to the elite), was to track and shoot a bull buffalo. Jeremy was game, and – accompanied by hunter Adrian Reed – set out with several photographers and 'officials' in tow. Undoubtedly the trap had been well laid, deceit and intrigue were rampant, and our hero in ignorant bliss. A fibreglass buffalo head, borrowed from the taxidermy store, stood concealed within a dense mopane thicket. Only the threatening form of the bossed horns could clearly be discerned.

Meanwhile the hunt continued. 'Fresh' spoor (made by an ashtray fashioned in the shape of a buffalo hoofprint) were discovered and followed. Two hours passed. It was hot and dusty, thorns tugged at their khaki clothing, every new tangle of bush held the prospect of action. Then 'Oxpeckers' (Black-eyed Bulbuls, actually) called, so surely the buffalo was close! Caution was paramount. Adrian and Jeremy inched forward, weapons at the ready. A hunt is always exciting and this was Jeremy's first. He was in a state of high tension. In the background, the entourage squirmed and grunted, strange behaviour that later could be correctly identified as desperate efforts to contain hysterical laughter. Adrian whirled Jeremy around. 'There it is! Shoot! Shoot!'

Jeremy whipped up his rifle and fired.

'You missed!' yelled Adrian, who then quickly loosed off a shot as well.

'Run, it's charging!' he bellowed at his fellow 'hunter'.

The two men turned and retreated. Jeremy covered a few paces before realizing all was not right. For one thing, his colleagues were writhing in mirth on the ground, and secondly the buffalo had remained entirely unmoved by the proceedings.

When the dummy head was inspected, Jeremy's redemption was found. His bullet had burned a hole neatly between its glass eyes!

# ADVENTURES IN THE ABYSS

## VICTORIA FALLS TO KARIBA

*Jumbo Williams*

IN A LETTER DATED 7TH SEPTEMBER 1900, Cecil John Rhodes expressed the wish that the railway should 'cross the Zambezi just below the Victoria Falls. I should like to have the spray of the water over the carriages'. Although he never saw the Falls and died three years before the railway reached them, his wishes prevailed over the strong aesthetic objections expressed at that time. The bridge was designed by Sir Douglas Fox and built out from each side of the gorge over a period of 14 months. The two halves were successfully joined on April Fool's Day in 1905 and the bridge officially opened that September. Two men died during its construction and yet another came close to the same fate. During the early phases of construction an engineer fell into the ravine and plunged about 30 metres before sliding to a halt upon a rock ledge. A derrick was rigged to support a strong light man and Jackie Whitten was lowered for the rescue. Unfortunately the rope was too short and needed to be lengthened by splicing, but by this time Jackie had lost his enthusiasm and refused to go down again. Eventually he succumbed to entreaties and exclaimed, 'Give me a good drink of whisky and I will try once more!'

Thus heartened and fortified by the fiery liquor, he heroically retrieved the severely injured man.

Crossing over the bridge to Zambia, Mike and I apprehensively studied the tempestuous Boiling Pot far below on our left and Second Gorge downstream to the right. Today we would follow a path of exploration which was only recently pioneered, and which even the intrepid Dr Livingstone was entirely denied. Sobek Expeditions, an American company which specializes in river rafting, launched a TV-publicized assault on the untamed wild water below the Falls on the 28th October, 1981.

On that day Richard Bangs, president of Sobek, dug hard with his oar-blades and pulled out of an eddy into the main flow above Rapid 1 – the Boiling Pot. The raft accelerated into the turbulence and careened beyond control straight into a rock face.

'Three metres from the wall I dropped the oars and held on. A blast of water pushed the boat up on its side, where it hung for a tense second ... then the boat plunged over, upside-down, into the rolling mess.' (R. Bangs, 1985).

Below the Falls, the Zambezi initially zigzags for about eight kilometres through four gorges before receiving input from the Songwe River. After this confluence it flows eastward for some 100 kilometres through the Batoka Gorge. In all the river descends 260 metres during this stretch, tumbling down more than 60 rapids and one waterfall. The cliffs at the base of the Victoria Falls are 110 metres high, while those at the downstream end of Batoka Gorge rise up 350 metres.

Mike and I rendezvoused with other passengers and together we hiked down the Palm Grove path to the Avon inflatables which were tethered adjacent the Boiling Pot. Once all were aboard our professional Sobek guides rowed upstream, hugging the shore and thus avoiding the swirling tentacles of current which could suck us into mid-river and toss the boat downstream like flotsam. I could hardly believe our situation. We were about to enter the very heart of the Falls, that 'awful chasm' so graphically described by Livingstone.

The blast from the Main Falls, as the tortured Zambezi slammed into its ancient foundations, drummed incessantly around us. It was impossible to

---

LEFT *The gorges below the Falls offer perhaps the world's best white-water sport.*
ABOVE *The continual spray nurtures a wealth of herbaceous flora.*

perceive much detail in the ravine which was dark with mist, but we could hardly fail to notice the frenetic river as it surged past us to escape these reverberating depths. I squinted upward against the light to the lip of the Falls and could see hurtling arrows of spray atomize completely in mid-flight. Immutable basalt towered above us to unconquerable heights. This was a giddy, surreal world of primeval black and white, an overwhelming surfeit of natural forces. Our boatman pulled strongly into a jumbled tongue of current and we lurched forward. Over the next seven days our world was to become an extraordinary combination of exhilarating action and scenes of remarkable beauty.

It does not take long to learn the essentials of survival as a passenger on a white-water raft. Momentum is the key, which implies the correct timing of the distribution of weight within the boat. This is termed 'highsiding' and distils down to enthusiastically flinging oneself around the craft from tube to tube. There are other niceties; how to bounce off a rock, what to do if overboard, and the correct method of righting an overturned boat. Certain functions are instinctively perceived to be appropriate; securing a firm grip, screaming during the descent, and gulping lungfuls of air before the watery wall engulfs one. The technicalities of actually deciding upon and maintaining a course through a rapid lie firmly on the tanned shoulders of the river guide.

Rapids 2 and 3 are small enough to permit some leeway in highsiding skills but the next two, 4 and 5, are demanding rapids of some historical note. During the first expedition the paddle-boaters portaged Rapid 4, and in Rapid 5 the same crew came too close to a 'pour-over' and fell into its hole. Grant Rogers, one of the two swept overboard, 'collided with a rock and then rolled over a metre-high fall' and was 'hauled to safety only barely conscious'. (J. Huckabay, 1987). He suffered three broken ribs and a pneumothorax which necessitated airlifting him by helicopter to Hwange hospital for treatment.

Fate was kinder to us and at the end of the first day we had safely negotiated ten rapids. Rapid 9 was portaged, as always. 'It was simply the largest rapid most of the party had ever seen.' (R. Bangs, 1985).

Our overnight camp was set at the mouth of the Songwe tributary. The one-day trippers climbed out of the gorge and returned to Livingstone while we re-stocked our rafts with additional supplies. Mike and I revelled in our luxurious roles as pampered tourists and enjoyed the opportunity to share experiences with other bush adventurers. Our guides were American or Zambian, while the six passengers came from Europe, Japan and Africa. Guide Kelly initiated the next day's action by leading the team into a roller-coaster swim down Rapid 10. Although a small metre-long crocodile occu-

LEFT *Sobek offer a seven-day rafting adventure that ends at the Matetsi River confluence. Moemba Cataract is the biggest obstacle to be negotiated. The falls will be drowned under the proposed Batoka Gorge Dam.*
RIGHT *Rapid 11.*

pied the rock pool behind the camp, we felt safe from any reptilian attack in the fast-moving water. Of course that may be entirely erroneous, but every-one survived. On the fifth day of Bangs' expedition, a crocodile sank its teeth into the back of one raft. After momentarily retreating when the tube exploded the crocodile attacked again and was only dissuaded from doing a great deal more damage when boatman John Yost slapped it with his oar. Fortunately there has not been another crocodile incident since then. We knew from experience that hippopotami represent a greater risk to boats, and the Sobek guides agreed.

During the second day we shot Rapids 11 to 19. It was a potpourri of superb action, sparkling water and harmless fun. Kelly missed her approach line at Rapid 18 and became the first on our voyage to flip over. However, Rapid 18 is generous in victory in that there is a deep placid pool down-stream to aid recovery of both craft and crew. We reached the sandy beach-

ABOVE *The craft is maintained on its course by the momentum generated by highsiders, the oarsman's skill and a liberal measure of good luck.*
ABOVE RIGHT *Rapid 18 is respected for its formidable 'hole', which has flipped over a good number of boats.*
OVERLEAF *'The Land of the Giants', Rapid 7.*

es of Bobo camp, our rest spot for the night, and had time to photograph the phenomenal scenery.

The Zambezi gorges change in character as one travels downstream. Above the Songwe confluence, the walls are uncompromisingly vertical and present sheer, bleak rock faces. This is a harsh environment, with vege-tation clinging precariously to cracks and ledges. A serial legacy of bygone falls, the switchback passage through the gorges limits one's view of what lies beyond or behind. Only from the air can one fully appreciate the topo-

graphy. This is the realm of the aerial raptors: Black Eagle and Augur Buzzard; Peregrine, Lanner and Taita Falcon. It also belongs to rock-nesting birds that feed on the wing; the swifts, martins and swallows. Ultimately though, it is the domain of Nyaminyami, Tonga deity of the Zambezi.

Below Songwe the gorges straighten out and become progressively deeper. The dark brown cliffs are faceted and often streaked red, pink and orange by rain-dissolved soil dyes. Because of the greater antiquity of these gorges, the sides are more weathered and less precipitous. This allows a wider range of fauna and flora the opportunity to become established. Consequently a deciduous woodland characterized by paper-bark trees (*Commiphora* spp. for example) encroaches down the lesser inclines, and candelabra-shaped *Euphorbia* trees stand neatly arranged on rocky shelves. We began to see diminutive klipspringers among the boulders, and baboons would bark alarm warnings whenever we floated by. Fan-shaped scars mark

the hillside where rock slides have gouged out a destructive trail to the river and a jumbled confusion of boulders lie strewn at the river's edge. Some of them must weigh hundreds of tonnes.

Even away from rapids, the Zambezi moves with purpose. The water is bottle green and flecks of foam often collect in the eddies. Water wells up from the deep, causing smooth circular patterns on the surface. Gradually these distort and vanish while still further rings emerge. There is the constant sound of restless water, falls giving a distant rumble and rapids a softer, lighter tone. When the river quickens near turbulence, the water turns turquoise and then frothy white with entrapped air. Within a rapid, a green tongue of laminar flow ('rooster's tail' to the boatmen) often indicates the best line to follow. Usually, however, the water is ultimately whipped into a true white frenzy. Banks of opalescent foam crash together, throwing showers of 'diamonds' into the sky. Long after the rapids are passed, air bubbles

still float up like some vast carbonated sea. In contrast to the river's hydraulics, the rocks are a sombre black, as monumental and inflexible as they have been for centuries.

The gorges are devoid of permanent human habitation and not without reason. Most of the river has remained inaccessible. The rugged desolation is striking and the environment tough, inhospitable and austere. Vince, a fellow passenger, termed it 'prehistoric', and so it is.

In 1860 Livingstone detoured from his route through the Batoka highlands for 'the promise of something grand'. However, he was unimpressed, '...we saw about 800 or 1 000 feet below us what, after Mosi oa Tunya, seemed two insignificant cataracts.' (D. and C. Livingstone, 1865).

These 'cataracts' were the Chimamba Rapids and Moemba Falls. At Chimamba the river is about 50 metres wide, and the flow is separated into two channels by a midstream obstruction. Using ropes we lined the empty rafts to near the edge of the seven-metre drop and then portaged around to put in below at an area of champagne effervescence.

Perhaps if Livingstone had climbed down to Moemba Falls, his impressions may have changed.

'Insignificant in height it's true, but when one stands on the brink of the lower cataract and sees the whole volume of the great Zambezi converging into a single pass only fifty or sixty feet in width, shuddering, and plunging for twenty feet in a massive curve that seems in its impact visibly to tear the grim basaltic rocks asunder, one learns better than from the feathery spray-fans of the Victoria Falls, what force there is in the river, and one wonders no longer at the profundity of the gorge.' (Lamplugh, 1908).

Moemba Falls obviously varies considerably, depending on the water level. We found them oriented on a northwest-to-southeast ledge, the water entering only on the extreme right (Zimbabwean) side and then immediately being forced by a stone face to divert left. Thereafter the river plummets into a highly agitated whirlpool and exits from view by executing a sharp dog-leg turn to the east. We camped both above and below the falls and spent two delightful evenings watching the silvery moonlight play on the dancing Zambezi.

On our fifth day of travel we drifted towards unmistakable evidence of industrial development. A cable hung suspended across the river and two rock tunnels had been blasted. We could see a road twisting up the escarpment and knew where it led, for we had previously driven along the upper sections of the same road.

This was the Batoka Dam site, final choice for the next hydro-electric scheme on the Zambezi. At the time of our journey, we did not know if construction was inevitable. If we had, I would perhaps have strived harder to absorb every geographical subtlety and each nuance of mood of this scin-tillating Zambezi. As it was, we greeted the Zimbabwean Army guards with a wave of the hand and drifted on.

A number of major rapids still lay ahead. 'Ghost Rider' was the biggest that we had to negotiate. The first time a descent was attempted it was dusk and two of the five boats capsized. One of the inflatables was then sent through unmanned and naturally sailed through with ease, hence the rapid's name. 'Deep Throat' presented the next obstacle. Here the Zambezi, two kilometres wide at the Falls, squeezes through an eight-metre constriction and then explodes against a rock wall. Bearing in mind the immense volumes involved, it is easy to appreciate the fearful undercurrents generated within the churning depths of 'Deep Throat'. In the past a guide who fell overboard was sucked down so far his eardrums burst. Lifejackets provide less buoyancy in such aerated water. For these reasons, the boatmen prefer to 'ghost' their rafts or ride the torrent with just one volunteer. Mike was aboard before our guide could finish pronouncing the word.

It seems to me one of the hallmarks of high adventure is reaching a point of no return, to be completely committed to the unknown that lies ahead. It is that realization which, as the raft accelerates along its one-way green highway to action, triggers a rise in adrenaline levels in the blood. The Zambezi's reputation as a premier white-water river rests not on the complex technicalities of its cataracts but rather on its volume and power. When a boat punches into the front stopper wave the highsiders are enveloped in spray and the bow of the craft buckles upward in protest. Then it feels as if some gigantic hand has seized the underside of the boat and is thrashing it about with titanic fury. Waves and whirlpools attack from every side; shaking, pulling and pummelling. The chaos switches within seconds. One moment there is a perpendicular liquid barricade, the next a void of spiralling disaster. Suddenly it is over, and one glides serenely on the crest of undulating waves. In common with all fine experiences, there is always a wistful yearning for just a little more.

After 'Deep Throat' the rapids are further apart. There is still 'Asleep at the Wheel', 'Wavetrain' and 'The Rock Garden', but generally the river slows down. There is time to dry out and savour the splendour and the majesty of this wild river of Africa.

We gently slipped along its dreamy waterway. For the first time since Mosi oa Tunya the Zambezi was silent, save for a murmur in response to the languid stroke of an oar. The October terrain looked scorched and withered, a merciless land of shadowless trees. We drifted past the dry ghosts of abandoned river beds. Black rock masses radiated back the shimmering heat. Near the river it was endurable, the water pleasantly cool due to the cold depths mixing with the warm shallows. We noticed more crocodiles now – on cue, as this stretch was called Croc Alley. Bird species increased in variety, and an African Fish Eagle attacked a White-crowned Plover. That night we shared our camp ground with a herd of grass-munching hippo.

After seven days our raft trip ended at the confluence of the Matetsi River and we drove back in a truck to Sobek's headquarters. However Mike and I

*The Zambezi is a big-volume river, famous for its velocity and surging power rather than the technical complexity of its rapids. Should you fall overboard, relax – the water is delightfully warm!*

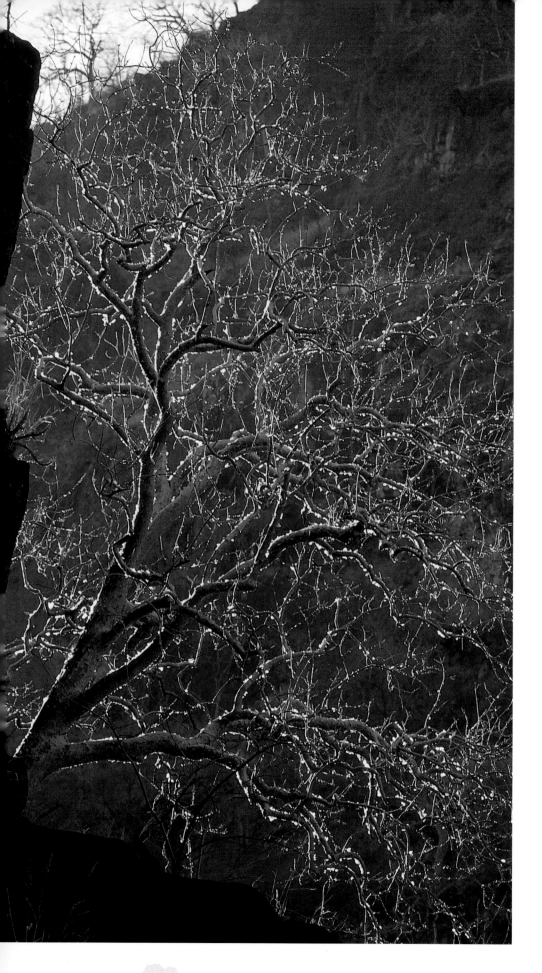

LEFT *An example of the paperbark tree* (Commiphora *sp.*).
ABOVE *Rafting the Zambezi is an amazing blur of exhilarating action, yet an abiding memory for many of the participants is the savage grandeur of those brooding gorges.*

soon returned, this time in our own rubber dingy, to complete the journey to Kariba. This section of the river really belongs to recreational fishermen, and resorts are established at both Msuna and Deka. The white water ends near Deka where there is a significant rapid, the last on the Zambezi until below Cahora Bassa Dam. Between Matetsi and Msuna the river remains primarily rocky but sandy nooks and *Phragmites* stands do occur. We chatted for a while with Zambians who had caught a few chessa. They told us the

police suspected there was marijuana trafficking across the river and recounted the story about one benevolent smoker who was trampled to death when he offered an elephant a drink of Coca Cola!

Beyond Msuna we entered Devil's Gorge, a steep-sided escarpment some 100-150 metres high. The topography is very broken, the result of erosion by rejuvenated Zambezi tributaries, and considered 'about the roughest country in the world'. (F.C. Selous, 1881). W.C. Baldwin, a hunter, agreed, 'The worst walking I have ever encountered.' (W.C. Baldwin, 1863). During that same period he also commented on his lifestyle, 'I am quite tired of this strong living – buffalo, eland or elephant day after day; I cannot eat quagga and the smaller varieties of antelope are awfully dry.'

Of course we merely floated on, quite unconcerned about the travails (past and present) of those on land. Within this savage valley, fairly close to the Gwaai confluence, we witnessed a phenomenal battle between two regal lords of the sky. A Martial Eagle swooped down before our eyes upon a hapless klipspringer and then almost immediately had to defend its kill from a Crowned Eagle. The combat occurred on the ground, both birds attacking with their outstretched talons, wings held open to help them maintain some balance.

Kariba came as an anticlimax. Devil's Gorge meekly opened into the drowned Milibizi River basin. Small waves lapped against the boat and a gull flew away. The lake seemed so empty and distant, it possessed none of the intensity of the Zambezi gorges. We boated to the Milibizi Hotel with the welcoming prospect of a cold beer.

# A SNARE FOR NYAMINYAMI

## LAKE KARIBA

*Jumbo Williams*

KARIBA DAM REMAINS AN impressive monument to man's engineering expertise and was, when completed in 1960, the largest dam ever built. The massive wall constrained the Zambezi spirit Nyaminyami and backed up a lake which is 220 kilometres long and, in places, about 30 kilometres wide. Nevertheless Kariba retained its wilderness character and remains richly endowed with scenery of untarnished splendour.

In fact, Kariba's beauty is so abundantly manifest that I suspect some residents have become almost unaware of the perfection around them. Vacationers come here for varying reasons. Many laze the day away sunbathing around the chlorinated pools of luxurious hotels and then try their luck at the casino during the balmy evenings. Others are attracted by the lake's reputation as a fisherman's Eden. Every year the annual tigerfish tournament receives hundreds of entries from all over Zimbabwe and Zambia. A fair number of visitors arrive hoping to escape from the trappings of routine and urbanization, and they either camp out by the shoreline or relax in the wilds at a safari lodge. Almost the entire length of the lake is game country. Many of these remote areas are best reached by boat, especially during the wet season when the dirt roads become quagmires.

Zimbabwe's Kariba town is the largest settlement by the lake. Its activities centre mainly around tourism and fishing, but also include the management of hydro-electric power installations. In addition, Kariba is a government administrative centre and a bridge route across the Zambezi.

It was obvious to us that a survey of the entire lake would be a tall order for our two-man expedition, especially in the few months allotted to the project. So we studied the maps and decided on several regions which seemed to be representative of the area's main geographical conditions and which were well away from the usual tourist haunts. Our mode of operation had to be altered considerably, for now we had to contend with storm-tossed waves rather than the Zambezi's relentless flow. Likewise, bird habitats were different and we found that we had to expand our scientific methods and classifications.

Milibizi village marks the upper limit of the lake, although in truth the transition from surging river to prosaic bulk of static water is discernible perhaps 20 kilometres further upstream. For reasons of logistics, economics and access we only explored the Zimbabwean lake shoreline and even with that limitation encountered a rich heritage of place names during our travels. Sebungwe, Binga, Chete, Ruzirhukuru, Sinamwenda, Sengwa, Kota Kota, Chalala, Bumi, Sanyati, Gache-Gache and legions of others, names that evoke the hills, river valleys and human endeavours that are long since drowned under the swollen Zambezi.

Before the Gwembe valley was flooded, almost 100 000 hectares of woodland were cleared to create snag-free zones for the envisaged commercial netting of fish. Trees were demolished by huge steel balls which were dragged by chains strung between powerful bulldozers. The resultant debris was burned and helped contribute to a super-abundance of nutrients when the lake was new. Fish populations soared and (contrary to predictions which favoured the *Labeo* or mudsucker genus) species of the Cichlid or bream family rapidly became the commonest type of fish. Tigerfish flourished as well, no doubt benefiting from the increased availability of their prey. During this time of plenty Zimbabwe's record tigerfish (15,5 kilograms) was landed. In addition to the species found naturally in the

LEFT *Can any visit to Kariba be complete without a boat trip out on the lake?*
ABOVE *Placid backwaters provide refuge for many aquatic species.*

Middle Zambezi, several other fish were introduced in order to enhance the commercial fishing possibilities. Greenhead Tilapia (*Sarotherodon macrochir*) were added as a deeper-water cichlid, and Kapenta (*Limnothrissa miodon*) were flown to Kariba in 1966-1967 from Lake Tanganyika. Kapenta are small sardines which shoal in deep open water, a niche not occupied by Zambezi fish species. Initially gill-netting rights were reserved for those tribes that traditionally lived by the Zambezi, but the project floundered and the fishing potential was not realized. Opportunities were then opened to commercial companies. In 1976, after some encouraging scientific trials, tenders for kapenta fishing were granted to individuals by the Rhodesian government. Since then this sardine species has formed the backbone of the fishing industry and is the basis of a multi-million dollar enterprise which supplies both Zambia and Zimbabwe with much-needed cheap protein.

Aquatic vegetation also blossomed in the young lake. A South American waterfern (*Salvinia molesta*) became a major concern when it choked up about one fifth of the lake's surface. In 1970 the species' natural regulator, a grasshopper (*Paulinia*), was imported and widely released, but the decline of the 'Kariba Weed' (now perhaps four per cent of the total area) was probably more attributable to wave action, fluctuations in water levels and a reduction of available nutrients. The plant was first collected on the Zam-

ABOVE *Kapenta are attracted to light and consequently all the fishing is done after dark with the aid of underwater and powerful surface lamps. The large circular net is winched up several times during the night. When a string of rigs lies offshore, the lake becomes a fairyland of dancing, bobbing lights.*
OPPOSITE *Around the time of the full moon, catches are generally poorer. Once ashore, the fish are sun-dried for several days on wire mesh racks and then bagged and shipped to markets.*
OVERLEAF *Ume Basin, Kariba.*

bezi at Katambora in 1949 and since then has extended upstream as well as downstream, for we initially noticed it at Mongu, in western Zambia.

Only a portion of the total shoreline was intentionally cleared of woodland and in many areas half-submerged hardwoods still stand. These naked forests are a distinctive Kariba feature, with their white-bleached limbs reaching skyward from the water as a gaunt testimony to endurance. They are a photographer's delight, visually complementing the angry blue of a thunderstorm or a sunset's vermilion haze. For the boat owner they are a nightmare. As the lake level drops areas formerly navigable become unsafe and many a craft has been holed. Obviously, we had to be very careful with our vulnerable inflatable.

The lake people net among the tree line, harvesting from the rich ecology of the shallows. They share this bounty with fish-eating species of waterbirds, particularly kingfishers, cormorants, darters and fish eagles. Kit Hustler is an ornithologist who, at the time of our visit, was based in Kariba town. His research brief was to assess the impact of darters and cormorants on the commercial fishing industry. Scant work had been done on these species in southern Africa's freshwater systems and he was collecting valuable information. The study was still in progress and conclusions premature, but Hustler's impressions were that the birds did not constitute a threat at all. We agreed that motivation for this research may represent an example of the imposition of prejudices onto another environment or culture. Project funding came from Scandinavia where fishermen and cormorants have long been feuding. If fish are becoming scarce, is not the problem due to excessive exploitation and environmental degradation? Why then try to grab the birds' slice of the pie? I hope Kariba never degenerates into this situation.

Kariba can be a very placid lake, mirror-smooth and wrapped in breathless haze. These are quiet moments when even time dissolves into infinity. Unfortunately that is not always the case. The surface can quickly rise into chaotic turbulence, with waves driven by winds blasting at 80 kilometres an hour. Sometimes the weather changes are predictable, but on other occasions thunderstorms sweep over the water at short notice, often catching boaters completely unawares.

Around mid-December we were counting waterbirds on the Bumi Hills floodplain and became perhaps a little too absorbed in our pursuit of unidentified snipe and nesting Redwinged Pratincoles. Eventually Mike perceived the wind quickening, indicating the approach of an afternoon storm. We hastened to 'Skimmer' moored nearby at the Bumi hotel jetty and faced what usually was, in calm weather, a 35-minute boat ride to our Tashinga camp. By the time we nosed out of the harbour, waves as high as two metres were rolling in from Kariba's Ume Basin. We realized the folly of braving such conditions and returned to safe refuge. As the afternoon passed, the weather abated slightly and with an hour of light remaining we again set out. Mike stood up in the front, trying to add weight forward as we nosed head on into the breakers. Inflatables are wet, uncomfortable boats but remarkably safe in rough conditions. 'Skimmer' was as buoyant as cork and responded instantly to a touch on the throttle. We felt confident of picking a way through the unpredictable wave pattern and were mainly concerned about puncturing on a submerged tree. After 30 minutes Mike checked our position. We were at least halfway and therefore decided to continue rather than turn back. Light was fading rapidly, extinguished by the tempestuous contorted sky, and we hardly glimpsed the white object which was drifting ahead near Tashinga's outer treeline. As we approached closer, another powerboat came crashing out of the Ume River mouth and stopped when its crew discovered what I could now identify as the overturned hull of a small craft. We arrived to find two tired middle-aged men in the water and assisted in their rescue. An attempt was made to secure the

half-submerged hull to a tree but without success because the waves were too violent. The shivering swimmers were placed in the Ume boat which then roared off into the twilight, their path illuminated by a powerful spotlight. Unfortunately, their skipper had evidently forgotten his promise to provide light and escort us home.

Night had descended with a vengeance. Our plans had not included dallying among the treeline for a salvage operation! We scanned the black featureless mass that was land, guessed where camp *could* be, and inched forward. This was not the best situation for a rubber inflatable. Our progress was by no means entirely under our control for we surged forward with each wave action. It was an eerie experience, the wind shrieking around us and thunder rolling. Trees materialized abruptly out of the gloom, loomed over our heads and then slipped by into darkness. For once our navigational skills were impeccable and we landed dead on target. What's more, although we had brushed a few stumps, 'Skimmer' was intact. As we had not seen any sign of the other rescue craft we thought it prudent to report the events to Russell Taylor, a Matusadona National Park research officer who lived at Tashinga. Mike had left his shoes in the boat, and as it was too pitch-black to find them, we piled into our Land Cruiser and drove to Russell's house. At this stage, the near tragedy turned into true comedy.

We parked at the rear of the Taylor's residence and walked in the dark towards the front door. Suddenly Mike yelled out in excruciating pain, violently flinging his arms starward and at the same time propelling our small flashlight and vehicle keys towards an unknown destination in the bush. He immediately began hopping about on one leg, executing an intricate series of tight circles and all the while firmly clasping the big toe of his other foot with both his hands. While able to ascertain from Michael's animated behavior and incoherent vocalizations that something terribly traumatic had occurred to my partner's bare foot, I had only the dull glow of a curtained window to aid my investigations. However even that disappeared.

'Buffalo!' cried Mike.

And sure enough, about four metres away and blocking out the window's light, was the steely eye and reflective wet nose of a buffalo. We hightailed it unannounced into the house, Mike athletically leading the way on his one leg. To our immense consternation and amazement, the buffalo followed us in!

Everything in life has an explanation. Mike probably stood on a scorpion because his foot ballooned up within minutes. The buffalo was an orphan and quite tame!

The Taylors were most sympathetic. Shortly afterwards the victims of the boat incident arrived, both feeling cold and exhausted. Their ordeal in the water had lasted two and a half hours and was initiated when a freak wave whipped up by the storm flipped their boat over. The lifejackets were irretrievably stowed away, so they had emptied the fuel containers and clung to these improvised flotation devices. As a result, one of the men suffered moderate chemical burns and was taken to hospital the next morning.

Russell was a university acquaintance from long ago. He had spent 13 years at Matusadona Park, studying aspects of its ecology and in particular the buffalo population. In Kariba's early years the lake's shoreline between the high- and low-water levels was barren and unproductive. This zone became colonized in about 1967 by a resilient evergreen grass that subsequently has made an important impact on the area's ecology. Torpedo grass (*Panicum repens*) forms thick matted swards and grows in luxuriant profusion by the water's edge. Four mammalian grazing species capitalized on this new fodder source: hippo, zebra, waterbuck and buffalo. Hippo have doubled in numbers in Russell's time, waterbuck are on the increase and in the past zebra were hardly ever sighted on the floodplains. However, it is the buffalo population that truly rocketed and yearly counts hardly indicate any slowing down of the current rate of growth.

LEFT *Drowned relics, these immersed treelines greatly increase the surface area available for colonization by algae and invertebrates. This, in turn, enhances the food resources which can be utilized by fish species.*

RIGHT *Kariba is able to satisfy the requirements of a wide spectrum of tourists. There are camping facilities, casinos, safari lodges, hotels, houseboats and luxury vessels. A car ferry plies between Mlibizi and Kariba town.*

LEFT *Elephants are often found drinking and bathing at the water's edge. A boat normally attracts very little attention and is an excellent way to watch big game.*
ABOVE *A hippo's hairless skin is kept soft and pliable by viscous, reddish glandular secretions. The animals cannot remain on land in bright sunlight for too long, or damage results. Even when in the water, they will occasionally submerge completely to keep the skin moist.*

The various animals utilize the panicum in different ways and do not necessarily compete. Hippo break off the foliage close to the ground, feeding almost exclusively at night. Buffalo are coarse grazers, opening up thick stands of grass and enabling other antelope which are close croppers (such as impala) to gain better access. Herds of over 1 000 buffalo are not uncommon and form an intimidating solid wall of black bodies and bossed upsweeping horns that probably deters most carnivores. Characteristically, the herds comprise dominant bulls, mature cows and their young, as well as adolescents. Older bulls are relegated to a rather solitary existence and are consequently more vulnerable to lion predation. These retired warriors spend their time resting in shady thickets, often cooling themselves at mud wallows or in the lake shallows. They can become short-tempered and unpredictable, perhaps as a result of the cumulative effect of flies, heat, old age and illness. Sometimes they have swollen 'knees' – buffalo suffer from brucellosis, a parasitic infection that can affect joints. Post mortems on herd outcasts suggest that they die of malnourishment, for their fat reserves are often severely depleted.

Matusadona Hills form part of the Zambezi escarpment and provide a

spectacular backdrop for the green picturesque plain that borders the Park shoreline. The Ume River enters the lake at the western border of Matusadona National Park and we were invited to join Lynne Taylor (Russell's wife) on a walk in this vicinity, the purpose of which was to see black rhino. Our guide for the outing was Sergeant Maxon, a veteran Scout with extensive bush experience. After following the spoor of several rhino for some hours, Maxon finally spotted a lone male resting in the shallows of a meandering Ume tributary. Unfortunately the wind was blowing our scent towards the animal and the four of us thus ducked out of sight and stealthily worked ourselves downwind. The rhino was situated at the base of a 10-metre-high eroded riverbank. We sneaked around the back of this cutting and advanced into a position directly above where the creature lay. Smugly confident of our canny tactics, we all leaned out over the edge and peered down, trying to locate our quarry. Only when Lynne gave a strangled squeak did I appreciate our miscalculation. Perhaps twelve paces behind us and scrutinizing our vulnerable posteriors in a vaguely myopic way, stood the black rhino. The situation was reminiscent of silent movie comedy. Here we were, caught between a substantial plunge into muddy slime and an inquisitive ton of shortsighted rhino. Following Maxon's example, we 'Pink-Panthered' a retreat along the lip of the cliff, trying as hard as possible to look just like any other mopane tree. The ruse worked, we escaped and the rhino ambled off into the thicket.

Maxon checked the wind direction and then started imitating a rhino's nasal-sounding call. Males are territorial – sometimes a pair will engage in deadly combat – and our fellow soon responded to the challenge. He approached with his head lowered, pawing the ground and kicking up an impressive dust cloud. It certainly convinced me! Whenever he came uncomfortably close, Maxon would become silent and merge into the vegetation. While our guide was thoroughly enjoying himself, I was battling with paroxysms of camera shake. Finally the rhino turned in disgust and confusion, and trotted away. Lynne had vanished, and we were a little concerned that she might be in the rhino's path. To our amazement, she descended miraculously into our midst. Earlier, Lynne had sensibly taken refuge up a tree. However by a quirk of fate the one she chose became a sort of maypole during our discourse with the rhino and she had enjoyed the action from an elevated centre-stage seat.

We spent a number of weeks at Tashinga before moving camp to near Chinga Cherere. This was an old Parks site, initially by the lake shore but now high and dry on account of the low water-level. There were two safari

LEFT *The Malachite Kingfisher is widely distributed along the Zambezi. We found a breeding pair at Matusadona and managed to rescue their offspring when the mudbank harbouring the nest tunnel collapsed and entombed the occupants.*
OPPOSITE *A Bennett's Woodpecker at the entrance of its nest in a dead mopane on the mainland shoreline opposite Fothergill Island. Usually three eggs are laid. The young will receive a diet of insects, primarily ants.*

enterprises nearby, both originally located on islands (Fothergill and Spur-wing) but at the time of our visit very much part of the mainland. Mike and I erected our tent beside a calm protected inlet that offered a magnificent panorama of the Matusadona range.

At the magical onset of evening when Africa's intense light assumes gent-ler hues, we would return to camp and soak the dust away in the hospitably warm lake shallows. Refreshed, we could relax and appreciate the seductive colours of sunset. Silhouetted mopanes stood watch beneath the out-stretched ruby-jewelled fingers that spanned the sky. Water lapped around their gnarled trunks and reflected a rippling path of gold. We would kindle a hardwood fire and sit quietly by its glow, alone in our thoughts at the pass of yet another peerless day. With the fall of night, resident hippo came ashore to graze and I would doze in my sleeping bag half-listening to the contented rhythm as they chewed.

This was also the season for storms, dark buffeting cumulus which swept grandly over the lake, gathering into thunderous banks of charged electrici-ty. Moist gusts flicked across our cheeks and whispered restlessly among the trees. The veld seems energized with anticipation. Ultimately this would be released with searing illumination and a rumbling explosion, then a tangen-tial onslaught of solid rain. Afterwards the delicious aroma of hot wet earth and an united chorus of bird, insect and amphibian song assailed the senses. Now it was a time of opportunity, feasts of plump termites, temporary drinking pools and fresh shoots of tender grass.

Mike encountered a pride of lions drinking at one newly formed pond of rainwater. Three of the cubs intercepted a solitary tortoise and converted the reptile into a whimsical plaything. Although intact, we never saw the shell move again – it seemed the sport was too severe.

We enjoyed Spurwing Island's hospitality on several occasions, quite unable to resist the facility of cold refreshments after a full day of tropical sun. Many anglers come to this Kariba resort in expectation of a battle royal with the lake's ferocious predator, the tigerfish, arguably the supreme fresh-water fighting prize. Before the rains the species congregates in estuaries, prior to moving upstream to spawn when the rivers flood. One well-known breeding area is the Sanyati Gorge, a short reach by boat from either Spurwing or Fothergill Island. Even now they say the Sanyati continues along its river bed, flowing under Kariba's surface to its old confluence with the Zambezi. During the famous Tigerfish Tournament (an annual event which is fiercely contested on the water by day, and around the hotel bars at night), the Sanyati becomes a frenetic boatway of optimistic fisherfolk.

Tigerfish are opportunistic and have successfully capitalized on the abun-dance of open-water shoaling kapenta. They are another example of a species which has flourished since the dam was completed. We regard Kariba as a successful enterprise. It provides considerable electric power to both Zambia and Zimbabwe, supports a thriving commercial fishing indus-try and has tourist potential which is still not fully realized. In addition the environment apparently has not suffered. The area adapted and retained

ABOVE *Adult waterbuck do not achieve the necessary physical status to establish and hold a territory until they are five or six years old. Territories are defended throughout the year. Serious fighting is fairly common and may even lead to the death of combatants.*

RIGHT *Tusks continue to grow in length and girth throughout an elephant's life. Unfortunately these modified upper incisors usually hasten the animal's demise - through the actions of ivory poachers. The impressive Churu bull lives within a national park, but that is no guarantee of safety.*

most of its wildlife and some species have positively blossomed. Kariba's broad expanse of water also confers some measure of protection to the black rhino from marauding Zambian poachers.

The local population has benefited from improvements in roads, communications and basic services. Burgeoning development has also increased job opportunities. People are now managing the area's natural resources

better and are gaining additional revenue through improved fish harvesting techniques, tourism and schemes like Campfire (*see* Concerns for the Future, p.171). However, the dam has now reached its maximum hydro-electric output and the strident call for more power has been raised. In Zambia the Kafue Dam presently adequately supplies that country, but in Zimbabwe the projected demand will outstrip output by 1995.

There are several options for new sources of electricity. Additional thermal power stations could be built, as Zimbabwe has extensive coal deposits. Cheap power could be imported from Cahora Bassa Dam if Mozambique managed to rid itself of civil war. Extensions are planned to both the north and south banks at Kariba. Two new Zambezi dam sites have been mooted, at the Mupata Gorge below Mana Pools and the Batoka Gorge which is 50 kilometres downstream of the Victoria Falls. Because the Middle Zambezi is topographically the most suitable portion of the river for dam construction, it has borne the brunt of this type of development. The Zambezi River Authority, a group established jointly by Zambia and Zimbabwe, has already drafted designs for a double-curvature concrete arch dam for the Batoka site. It will be 196 metres high and 600 metres across, and thus dwarf the 128-metre high structure at Kariba. However, while the latter holds some 156 billion cubic metres of water, the Batoka Dam would contain a mere two billion cubic metres. Ecologically, it seems the Batoka Dam will have significantly less impact than the Mupata alternative. The gorges upstream of Batoka are very steep and the Zambezi will continue to be confined within them. Flooding will be minimal in comparison to Mana's flat *Acacia albida*-forested valley, which would be almost entirely submerged. (Mana Pools National Park has been declared a World Heritage Site by the United Nations.)

Because of the incised nature of the Batoka terrain, few islands will be created and it is unlikely that significant numbers of animals will be trapped as the water rises. There are relatively few species that will be substantially affected by the dam. We know Rock Pratincole are likely to be one of the unfortunates. We counted 706 individuals in the stretch between Victoria Falls and Kariba Dam, of which 106 were in the area to be flooded. This represents five per cent of the estimated total number of Rock Pratincole for the Upper and Middle Zambezi, a river distance of about 1 830 kilometres. The altered flow may affect breeding success below the dam, although the species does form colonies downstream of Kariba. Rock Pratincole breed at natural lakes further north in Africa, but there are no reports of the birds adapting to Kariba Dam and it is unlikely that they would do so at Batoka. There are several raptors which breed in the Falls gorges, the Taita

LEFT *Which way to the zoo? That may be the only safe place left for the black rhinoceros, which has been hunted to the brink of extinction. The Middle Zambezi was one of the last sizeable refuges remaining, but it appears as if anti-poaching efforts have, unfortunately, not been able to match the poaching pressure.*
RIGHT *Chete Gorge, Kariba.*

LEFT *Lake Kariba shoreline.*

ABOVE *Kariba Dam was completed in 1958 and presently is the third largest in Africa. The Zambezi provides 78 per cent of the lake's annual water gain, secondary rivers 14 per cent and local rainfall eight per cent. Most of the water lost from Kariba flows through the turbines.*

Falcon being the rarest and most famous. Others include Lanner and Peregrine Falcon and Black Eagle. It is thought they will be minimally affected by the hydro-electric project, perhaps not at all.

There are very few tribesmen living in the vicinity of the proposed dam and those who do are fishermen and unlikely to lose their livelihood as a result of the Batoka scheme. Businesses should flourish as the dam is close to the main Bulawayo-Victoria Falls road and a steady stream of Falls tourists can be anticipated. Marinas, hotels and the fishing industry (including kapenta) are expected to benefit substantially. River rafting will be severely impacted as a result of the scheme, but hopefully not entirely eliminated.

The Victoria Falls gorges provide a spectacular experience for the intrepid and we encountered nothing quite like them during our expedition. The dam will mean the irrevocable loss of another wild sliver of Africa, the further disfigurement of a magnificent river. Man's concrete masterpieces will never match the splendours of nature. Planners would do well to heed the lessons of earlier schemes. Kariba for example, has so much stored potential backed up behind its wall and yet limited capability for further turbines to usefully harness the energy. Cahora Bassa has never generated any significant amounts of electricity as it has been sabotaged for more than a decade.

The Zambezi must not slip into the ignominious fate that befell many of America's wild waters – an endless procession of artificial obstructions which have all but stilled the life force and currents of those once mighty rivers.

# THE VALLEY

## KARIBA WALL TO RUKOMECHI

*Jumbo Williams*

AFTER ESCAPING THE CONFINES of Kariba Dam, the Zambezi continues as an international border for a further 300 kilometres before entering Mozambique. For most of this stretch the river courses within the secluded and inaccessible 'Zambezi Valley', guarded on both sides by the towering hills of a stark, inhospitable escarpment. The land abutting the southern bank is preserved by Zimbabwe's National Parks Department and has gained international renown as a wonderful pristine wilderness. On the opposing Zambian bank a slightly different situation prevails. Part of the basin is occupied by subsistence fishermen and farmers while the remaining portion is managed by government wildlife authorities.

A strange paradox exists, because this diverse natural ecosystem relies for its life force on a river whose flow is directly regulated by the electricity demands of settlements far beyond the Zambezi's valley. Kariba's floodgates have not opened for a decade, so all the water immediately downstream of the wall has gained tortuous passage through the turbines and its volume is determined by hydro-electric requirements. Thus the river's level drops over weekends when industries close and usually peaks during mid-week. It even fluctuates on a 24-hour basis, as we were soon to discover.

Mike and I pulled out of Kariba town and ascended the winding hill-flanked road to Makuti. From there we drove to Marongora camp which is based at the edge of the impressive escarpment. We paused a while, gazing

north towards Zambia, and could distinguish the distant Zambezi glinting through the dry-season haze of dust and veldfire smoke. From almost beneath our feet the hillside plummeted recklessly downwards for a thousand metres or more and merged below with the flat valley floor.

We turned off the main road and descended the escarpment via an older, rougher route, heading for Nyamuomba Island which lay in the extreme west of our view. The electric atmosphere of the Zambezi hit us with a hot surge of excitement. The area was not new to me as I have made many visits there, but still the emotion gripped like a fever. The sultry aura affirmed a subconscious realignment into a world of primeval references and survival-honed reflexes. One has to observe nature's laws and mind her ways. Political opinions and fat credit cards carry no weight here. I suppose all humans taste the same to a crocodile.

Nyamuomba is a National Parks station. Ranger Mark Brightman was in charge and he assigned us an excellent campsite which offered good midday shade. We pitched tent and moored our boat close by on a small sandy beach. That evening Mike and I happily rocked back on our canvas easy chairs, well satisfied with our new home. A pair of Giant Eagle Owls began their sonorous hoots and further away the sawing rasp of a leopard echoed down the night-clad hillside. Nyamuomba was important to our studies, for here the Zambezi undergoes an abrupt change in character and in the habitat types it supports. After being released from the dam, the river hustles for some 20 kilometres within the sheer Kariba Gorge. Then, a few metres upstream from our evening fire, it slows down and expands over a flat alluvial plain. Unlike the gorges below Victoria Falls which gradually recede from the river, here the escarpment takes its leave of the Zambezi without so much as a single glance back at its former companion. We wondered

LEFT *Out of the water, hippopotami establish pear-shaped territories which the male defends against intruders. The territories are marked by piles of faeces which are scattered over bushes or stones by a flicking side-to-side movement of the animal's short, flattened tail.*
ABOVE *Free spirit.*

115

whether the sudden topographical change would be dramatically mirrored in the distribution of wildlife species.

Our ambience of contentment disappeared with the first light of morning. I glanced out of habit down to 'Skimmer' at the water's edge. The inflatable was gone! Hearts pounding, we raced to the beach. The craft was nowhere to be seen but we found fresh hippo footprints in the sand around where it had lain. We were nonplussed. Could an inquisitive beast have nudged 'Skimmer' afloat? There was a Zambian fishing settlement on the opposite bank and they would have good use for a boat and motor. As it was, their relations with Zimbabwe Parks were poor; Mark regularly confiscated their fishing nets when he found them within Zimbabwe's territory. 'Skimmer' was essential; without it our expedition was over. We went to inform the ranger and our despondency deepened as the full impact of the catastrophe began to sink in. Mark was full of smiles when he met us. I guess he read our faces. Yes, he knew the whereabouts of our inflatable, it was not far downstream, high and dry on a sandbank.

'Had we secured our boat with a rope? The river fluctuates a lot here.'

We had not. It was a mistake we never repeated as the lesson was too traumatic. Logically, the effects of turbine flow should be greater at Nyamuomba than anywhere downstream. The narrow gorge accommodates a volume increase by significantly raising its water level, and in addition there are no major tributaries entering the Zambezi between Kariba and our camp which could diminish the 'tides'. We were fortunate that 'Skimmer' drifted to shore so soon, as it could have floated on for kilometres. With Mark's help we recovered the craft and boated upstream, waving enthusiastically at the Zambians in penance for our unjustified dark suspicions.

Kariba Gorge's avifauna fitted the pattern we had come to expect from this type of topography. Black Eagles exploited the blustery updrafts close to the vertical rock faces, twisting and swooping as they searched out dassies, their favourite prey. At a much higher altitude a Black Stork spiralled effortlessly in slow descent. This is one of the few places in Zimbabwe where they are known to breed. African Fish Eagle nests seemed quite prevalent, usually located in trees with a commanding river view. As we progressed towards the dam, the water was initially silky-green and very deep. Occasionally, the frenzied thrash of feeding tigerfish broke the surface's serenity, hinting at a harsh, highly competitive piscean struggle for survival. In this part of the Zambezi only a few quiet shallows are available for small fry to gain refuge from predators. Fishermen come to the gorge in search of big tigerfish, and also for another sport fish, the vundu, a member of the catfish family. This bottom-dwelling giant can weigh in excess of 50 kilograms. Strangely, cheap strong-smelling soap is an excellent bait. Unlike the acrobatic tiger, vundu stay deep when hooked, usually setting off downstream in a headlong rush of power that has the angler hotfooting it along the bank in an effort to maintain some line on the reel.

*Replete with buffalo meat, this lioness rests by the cool river.*

The hillsides around us were a mixture of jumbled boulders and precipitous rock cliffs, between which was interspersed a precarious woodland that clung tenaciously wherever it could gain hold. On the borders of this vegetation we observed quite a number of bushbuck and a few regal kudu. Nearer the dam the river became decidedly more lively, although still within the capability of 'Skimmer'. We rounded a corner – and the wall, looming immense and immutable, confronted us and filled our vision. After a reconnoitre, we manoeuvred closer to photograph the inflatable against the concrete backdrop. Suddenly a most penetrating and urgent whistle reverberated around our heads. The source was an officious-looking fellow, attired in an all-white uniform, standing atop the wall. He gestured wildly in a manner which left no doubt that he was considerably irked, that we were in forbidden territory and committing a crime of heinous magnitude. In this part of Africa any dam or bridge may be regarded as a potential target for sabotage and consequently camera activity is frequently forbidden. We

retreated in hasty disarray, still to the piercing accompaniment of the extremely agitated guard's whistle.

The downstream portal to the gorge is delineated by a stout pair of vertical rock pillars. Drifting beyond them one's vista explodes horizontally; the river relaxes, spreading to gently encompass several flat sandy islands. On these, salmon-pink hippo sunbask in communal comfort. A fringe of lush green reeds dances to the caprice of swirling currents while kingfishers dart in the air above the rippling shallows; shimmering dashes of brilliant colour against the uncluttered azure sky.

ABOVE *Crocodiles are dangerous. Take care when you swim in the Zambezi!*
RIGHT *Buffalo drink water regularly, generally twice daily, and are inclined to graze in its vicinity, often using the shelter of extensive reedbeds in which to rest. They regularly wallow in mud, an activity which is important in regulating their body temperature.*

LEFT *Lions hunt predominantly at night. Males take little part in the procedure, leaving this to the females, but are quick to feed once the kill is made. The lionesses may then have to wait for their meal until the dominant lion has eaten his fill. Hyaenas (*ABOVE*) will lurk in the shadows, hoping to snatch an unguarded morsel when the opportunity presents itself.*

After several excursions downstream, it became obvious to us that there were marked differences between the northern and southern banks. The Zimbabwean land is state-owned, designated for safaris and game management. There were no permanent settlements other than those for National Parks staff. Across in Zambia the river was lined with a succession of small rural Tonga villages built in the traditional pole-and-daga style. The people's main occupation was fishing, although they also grew some vegetables and maize and kept small numbers of domestic fowl, goats and cattle. It was a rural subsistence existence; they relied on the river for food, drinking water and ablutions.

The contrasting land usage was reflected in the state of the environment.

The Zambian shore was overgrazed, bare and eroded; much of the woodland had been cleared for agriculture or for firewood. A dense, almost continuous stand of aquatic vegetation lined the bank. We saw no wild animals,
only malnourished cattle. In contrast, the Zimbabwean land provided an
endless parade of game and the deciduous *Colophospermum mopane*-dominat-
ed woodland was well-established. Erosion was absent or minimal. There
was much less aquatic growth along this shoreline and in our view this can be
attributed to the disparity in hippo distribution. On our expedition we routinely counted all the hippo we saw, and on this stretch of the river only
noted one animal on the Zambian side compared to 319 along the
Zimbabwean bank. Any hippo grazing on the northern side stood a good
chance of ending up in the pot. Survival had determined their grazing range
and the consequent impact on the vegetation. This in turn had affected the
distribution of reed-dwelling creatures, both in and out of the water.

Unlike hippopotami, the distribution of crocodiles appeared similar on
both sides of the river. From our Nyamuomba camp we could watch
Zambian fishermen wading chest deep to place their nets around likely
bream locations. Fish form a large percentage of a crocodile's diet and we
had personally seen some monster crocodiles basking near the fishing areas,
so it seemed quite conceivable to us that these men were in mortal danger.
Certainly, should a crocodile attack, they would be severely disadvantaged at
that depth of water. Their safety, they amiably assured us, was guaranteed. A
witchdoctor was hired to place a protective spell over the fishermen and for
years now not one attack had occurred.

Mike and I had some inkling of a crocodile's strength. At Luangwa, an-
thrax struck in the national park and the hippo population suffered terribly.
It was a sobering demonstration of power to watch crocodiles bite hunks of
carcass flesh and then rapidly spin about their long axes in order to tear away
the meat. Crocodiles also earned our respect for their stealth and wary manner. We set up for two days at a popular mudbank in order to photograph
the creatures. Finally one three-metre prospect glided into focus. Three
clicks of a Nikon shutter, a hurried tail-flick, and our subject disappeared.

Sometimes familiarity does breed contempt. Some safari companies offer
canoe trips on the Middle Zambezi and a guide for one of these allowed his
group to swim in less than ideal conditions. A crocodile seized a young boy
and would most certainly have killed him had an adult passenger not attacked the animal, thrusting his hands into its mouth and prizing open the
jaws. The crocodile thrashed and spun, avulsing the man's arm, but both of
the victims survived. It was not the first time people had swum in this area,
so perhaps the reptile had been anticipating a meal.

LEFT *The dazzling Carmine Bee-eater is a gregarious intra-African migrant which
breeds in the vertical banks of low-lying tropical river valleys. Sometimes an entire
colony is lost when the Zambezi erodes and collapses a riverbank.*
RIGHT *Whitebreasted Cormorants are relatively uncommon on the Zambezi and
yet breed in large numbers on one of its tributaries, the Kafue River.*

123

The main road linking the capital cities of Zimbabwe and Zambia bridges the Zambezi at Chirundu. We made our next base at this tiny border settlement which is one of the easier places for visitors to access the river. Our friends, Fanta and Lesley, kindly offered the use of their cottage. For us Chirundu was a polluted eye-sore. Refuse lay scattered everywhere, there were no basic amenities available to campers nor even a designated campsite. The area was a warren of bush roads and generally remained in a state of post-war disrepair. Basically, Chirundu was quite unprepared for the hordes of weekenders that periodically descended into the valley on public holidays. I feel the town definitely needs to be included in any overall regional development plan. Not that the animal life has retreated! While sipping thirst-quenching pilseners on the veranda of the Chirundu Hotel, Mike and I watched an elephant family of four unconcernedly slaking their thirst with water from the swimming pool.

Rukomechi, the next downstream port of call, presented a marked contrast to our Chirundu impressions. This privately leased luxury camp was idyllically located where the seasonal Rukomechi Stream enters a broad sweep of the mother Zambezi. Buildings were mainly reed and thatch and they blended in harmoniously with the natural surrounds. The safari camp was immaculately kept. Its manager at the time was Garth Thompson, a recognised expert on the African bush, and he kindly permitted us to pitch our tent on his property. We established ourselves a bit downstream in an attempt to be unobtrusive. Rukomechi is one upmarket example of what can be provided for the tourist on the Zambezi; there are other equally good enterprises elsewhere. Basic comforts are well cared for – not an easy task in this remote setting. Electricity was generated by diesel motors, all the food and drinks were transported on rough dirt roads, shade temperatures in excess of 40 °C continually threatened to melt the ice in the refrigerators. Guests had several outdoor options with which to occupy their time; daily game viewing, either by vehicle or on foot, or excursions on the water by canoe or powerboat. Clients were always accompanied by an experienced guide.

In Zimbabwe there are strict laws regulating the qualifications of these personnel. For example, a professional guide is examined not only on his factual knowledge of the environment, but also on his practical ability to kill dangerous animals; indeed, some of the operators are licensed professional hunters. It can be a comfort when walking in the wilds to know one's leader is competent to deal with big game. We never carried weapons. We travelled in places where suspicion of foreigners ran high and the observance of human rights were sometimes fragile. The military defined the law. If guns had been found during the many personal searches we endured, these memoirs would have been written from within some dank prison. So in the bush we trusted on good luck, the Lord, and common sense.

*Rukomechi Camp lies upstream of Mana Pools National Park in an idyllic area, rich with bird and animal life. Elephant and lion wander close to the camp. Here Jumbo lost a pair of binoculars to hyaenas.*

125

# WILD PLACES

## MANA POOLS TO KANYEMBA

*Jumbo Williams*

AFTER RUKOMECHI WE MOVED to Mana Pools, a game reserve that thoroughly deserves its long-standing reputation as a wildlife paradise. The allure of Mana is directly attributable to its unique vegetation which forms the foundation of a complex inter-relationship between the river, the trees and many animal species. The region's floodplain consists of rich alluvial soils, deposited over aeons by the meandering Zambezi. And meander it does, for oxbow lakes (which give the reserve its name) exist several kilometres from its present course.

We met Kevin Dunham who had studied Mana's ecology for five years and he explained to us some of its mysteries. A common tree is *Acacia albida*, a thorn species 10 to 30 metres high and with the classical shade-providing umbrella shape. The park's floodplain woodland can be classified into pure *A. albida*, *A. albida*-dominated, and mixed woodland stands (there are also some other types, depending on the soil and topography). *A. albida* is a pioneer species. It is fast-growing, perhaps 25 centimetres a year, and is able to tolerate sandier soils than many of the other woodland species. This property allows the plant to colonize infertile sandbanks and thus stabilize them and reduce erosion. With time, humus collects and more clay-like soils are deposited so that the earth becomes richer and better able to support other types of trees. Gradually there is a transition from pure *A. albida*, through *A. albida*-dominated intermediates, to a totally mixed woodland. The latter represents the climax vegetation and areas can be aged – in terms of when they were colonized by trees – by the type of forestation. This, in turn, gives an indication of how the river's path has altered over the years.

LEFT *A quiet moment on the river.*
ABOVE *Chacma baboon surveying his domain.*

How does all this affect the animals? *A. albida* is colloquially known as the 'Apple-ring tree', for the fruit resembles the coiled skin of a peeled apple. It is remarkably nutritious, with a high percentage of protein, and is produced in the dry winter months when food is scarce. During these times pans in the central sections of the valley dry up and elephants residing there move to the greener river belt to feast on the *A. albida*. The fruit then constitutes a major portion of the elephant's diet. The story does not end there, however. Elephants have a rather inefficient digestive system and some 40 per cent of the material eaten can pass through intact. Viable seeds are thus dispersed by these far-ranging giants, allowing the acacias to establish in new places. In addition, animals as diverse as guineafowl and Chacma baboons search through the dung for edibles.

We settled in at Mana's Nyamepi camp which is situated within a mature *A. albida* grove. Only 50 vehicles were permitted in the reserve at one time in order to limit tourist pressure on the facilities and the environment. The Park has some unusual laws. Visitors are free to walk wherever they wish, but a pamphlet reminds one that wild animals are dangerous and that the authorities cannot be held responsible for any injuries or damage. This precautionary statement was warranted, for about six bull elephants routinely fed within the camp grounds.

Warden Cousins explained that it takes about two years for the elephants to become accustomed to the presence of humans. Generally the neighbourhood goliaths behave like true gentlemen, which is fortunate as most campers pitch their tents under the shady acacias. We were amazed at the care exhibited by the elephants when around camp. For example, even at night they would detour around our abode rather than break a thin clothes line strung from the tent to a fruit-laden tree. Their movements were in-

credibly nimble and quiet. Only once did an elephant come uncomfortably close, when it stumbled over our guy ropes and inadvertently brushed against the tent and a leg of one of our guests.

Mazoe was a different matter altogether. A mature male and camp regular, he was named after a citrus company on account of his unequivocal partiality for oranges. Once he had sniffed their tantalizing fragrance there was little that could stop Mazoe. Tents were pushovers and boats reduced to splinters; only concrete structures kept him out. Mazoe's addiction was directly the result of irresponsible human behaviour: perhaps someone fed him initially or left food lying around for him to sample. Parks staff placed a collar around his neck so tourists could recognize him and take precautions.

However, Mazoe knew a trick or two and he tried his favourite food-acquiring ploy on a friend of ours, Alastair Chambers. Al was a professional guide, dedicated to his work and well respected by his peers. One afternoon he had just arrived and was setting up camp. Mazoe was close by and obviously had decided to rout the new arrival and take the pickings of whatever delicacies were left abandoned. He chose the wrong man. Al had his back to the elephant and did not see Mazoe initiating his intimidating charge. We yelled a warning but by then Mazoe was already hurtling along with im-

pressive momentum and speed. Chambers turned, with the behemoth bearing down upon him from some 10 metres away.

'Don't be childish!' he yelled sternly, firmly clapping his hands as if impatiently rebuking a five-year-old child. The effect was instantaneous. Mazoe skidded to a humiliating halt and even before the ensuing shower of dust had settled on Chambers' shoulders, Al had disdainfully turned his back on the mortified elephant.

Of course the close proximity of such sizeable creatures can make a different impression on lesser mortals. At one time our neighbours included a middle-aged couple. Unfortunately the hapless wife was hopelessly petrified by the elephants' gigantic presence and after two nights sans sleep they abandoned their adventure and went home.

There are many stories about Mana, as can be expected when unrestricted movement is permitted within the domain of big game. Every night we could hear lion setting off on their nocturnal hunts. Honey badgers and hyaenas would scavenge around the tents. Old buffalo, ousted from the herd, grazed the *Panicum* that grew thick at the water's edge. We were lucky enough to see three cheetah, lean athletes of the African bush and uncommon at Mana. One male had an injured hind leg. Perhaps the other two cats provided their companion with food, for it seemed in reasonable condition. We reported the lame animal to Kevin Dunham, but he said park policy was not to interfere. (Later we heard the animal had died.)

We also experienced a memorable sighting of an altogether different nature. I was in camp with a friend, the footloose entrepreneur Aiden 'Oinks' Hogg, while Mike was in Zambia trying to obtain research permits. As mentioned earlier, safari companies of ten conduct canoe excursions down portions of the Middle Zambezi. One of the guides, Tim, told us of an African Skimmer's nest situated downstream of Mana, and Oinks and I set out to investigate the truth of report.

'If you can't find it, don't worry. I will be canoeing down later with clients,' said Tim.

We also experienced a memorable sighting of an altogether different nature. I was in camp with a friend, the footloose entrepreneur Aiden 'Oinks' Hogg, while Mike was in Zambia trying to obtain research permits. As mentioned earlier, safari companies often conduct canoe excursions down portions of the Middle Zambezi. One of the guides, Tim, told us of an African Skimmer's nest situated downstream of Mana, and Oinks and I set out to investigate the truth of report.

A scan through powerful binoculars confirmed both Tim's presence and Oinks' observation and we set off in hot pursuit. Now it should be remembered that many months had passed since either of us had visited civilization or had the pleasure of the fairer sex's company. In fact it would be a reasonable assumption that our testosterone surges were in those moments escalating to levels at least comparable to a bull elephant in full musth. There was scant attempt by the ladies to cover up at our approach. Tim was in a sublime state. His eyes appeared glazed over and vague, and the benign greeting he gave us suggested he was indeed in raptures and beyond responding to our interruption. We stuck to the party for the rest of the day like dried mud on a buffalo's hide, until a golden-hued sky at last prompted our reluctant journey home.

Oinks departed, Mike arrived and we left Mana by road for Chewore. Now we travelled in thick 'jesse', an impenetrable bush entanglement which is prevalent within the Zambezi Valley. The temperatures soared unabated and the drive became laborious with tsetse flies continually feeding upon us whenever our vehicle became stuck. The sand was very soft and 'Whimbrel' over-loaded, so it came as no surprise when we sank axle-deep while crossing Sapi's parched broad river bed. Using a handsaw we cut some timber struts to place in the sand for wheel traction. We disconnected the trailer,

raised the truck with a 'Tanganyika' ladder jack, inserted the logs underneath and similarly lined the path ahead. Then we would drive ahead as far as we could (perhaps five metres) before again sinking down. The trailer would then be hand-winched up to the truck, using the towbar as an anchor, and the whole procedure repeated. Not that we minded, for a pack of 15 rare wild dogs had ambled out of the jesse to watch our pedestrian progress.

Our destination was Mwanja hunting camp, a concession owned jointly by the Rosenfels and Joubert families. They had generously granted us permission to use their property as our base. Although Mike and I have no desire to hunt, we do not object to the controlled exploitation of the Zambezi's game for this purpose. Wildlife in Africa must be made as profitable as possible in order to justify the financial commitment its conservation requires. Safari hunting is a remunerative business and, if anything, is likely to increase animal numbers by decreasing the activities of poachers: as each trophy represents considerable profit, hunting operators are less inclined to be lax and allow someone to pilfer their livestock. It has been calculated, for example, that an elephant shot legally for sport yields five times more money than the same individual would when poached. In addition, that money is legitimately declared and is thus taxable; it also brings foreign currency into the country.

Hunting quotas are government-regulated in most Zambezi countries and each company is apportioned a certain number of animals. At Mwanja camp the clientele was very international: South African, American, German, Italian, Arabian, English and French, to mention a few. During our stay Dick arrived, an American who had made his money in real estate. This was his second visit to Africa and his main quest was trophy ivory. Along the Zambezi the average size of tusks increases as one travels east, hence his chances of success were perhaps better at Mwanja than elsewhere in Zimbabwe. However, as he was warned, big elephants are hard to find and require a lot of effort. Dick was very enthusiastic and began each day with gusto. Against the advice of Dave Joubert, his professional hunter, he continually bared his head and shoulders to the sun and by the third day of hard tracking in the escarpment foothills was ill with sunstroke and dehydration. We bade him goodbye while he was recuperating. I think Dick was a little concerned about our frugal lifestyle and tatty appearance, for he presented us with some of his old T-shirts as a farewell gesture.

We wasted no time in heading upstream, motoring to the lower Mana Park boundary where another tourist camp, Chikwenya, was established. This was run by Jeff Stutchbury, a grand old Zambezi character who had pioneered the wilderness safari concept on Kariba long before the others that followed. Although we were within our research rights to boat in the area, we respected Jeff's crusty temperament and strong territorial instincts. Besides, we wished to greet the man and tap his vast experience and knowledge. He met us at Chikwenya's harbour and immediately took us under his wing. Chikwenya was a collection of thatched-roof constructions, with cement walls tastefully concealed and the whole complex tucked away to the point of invisibility within *C. mopane* woodland. National Parks used Chikwenya as a base for anti-poaching operations, for it had an airstrip, radio communications and the firm support of Stutchbury himself.

The place was alive with activity when we arrived – a group of rhino poachers had crossed from Zambia into the Chewore region. The alarm was sounded when hunters discovered the intruders' cached property and a combined Parks and police unit set up an ambush to intercept them on their return. Unfortunately, not enough men were available to cover all approaches and when the poachers did arrive it was by an unexpected route. In the ensuing gunfire one poacher died, but the leader escaped with some of his accomplices. They had killed two rhino.

It soon became clear that the leader was well versed in anti-tracking methods. Most likely he was a former 'freedom fighter' who had received training in guerilla warfare. He headed west, repeatedly returning to the Zambezi to conceal his tracks. Apparently he once even floated downstream for some distance before re-entering the bush. The trail turned lukewarm. Parks used spotter aircraft and also installed stop-groups along the poachers' anticipated line of flight, yet the hunted men still found the time to slaughter three more rhino. At this stage they were known to be in the vicinity of Chikwenya. Troops were stationed at likely crossing points with instructions to shoot

OPPOSITE Acacia albida *woodland, dry-season home of Mana elephants.*
ABOVE *The honking call of Egyptian Geese is a familiar riverine sound. These birds spend much of their day loafing on the shoreline. When breeding, they often use the abandoned nests of other species such as Hamerkop, lining the nest hollow thickly with down.*

anyone moving on the river at night. It seems that in the heat of the chase they had forgotten our little expedition. (No-one else could legally be on that stretch of river.) Jeff absolutely forbade us to leave and offered food and accommodation. Who could refuse an invitation like that? We dined with Chikwenya's tourists and a few of the Parks staff joined our company. Their stubbled faces were lined with fatigue and drawn taut with determination and smouldering anger. Jeff Stutchbury personally walked us to our cottage. Over the years there had been several lion attacks on humans in camp – with one fatality – and it was policy never to leave guests unescorted when they walked to their chalets at night.

The poachers finally escaped. They stole into Chikwenya and used a camp boat to flee back to Zambia. Subsequently four Parks members went over to the opposite shore and reclaimed Jeff's property. For this action they were arrested by Zimbabwean police and incarcerated. Representations to the government minister responsible for Parks, and efforts by Glen Tatham, finally secured their release. As could well be anticipated this regrettable bureaucratic bungle did not improve the morale of those people who were daily risking their lives in anti-poaching activities (we personally spoke to the men after their release).

With stomachs replete and morale buoyant we gratefully bade Chikwenya farewell and launched 'Skimmer', floating placidly downstream so as to conserve our outboard fuel. The Zambezi is several kilometres wide at this stretch and we opted to concentrate on the northern shoreline, which we had not investigated during our upward journey from Mwanja. We felt relief by immersing ourselves in nature's fascinations and temporarily escaping the traumatic realities of its preservation. Here the Zambezi continued the same idyllic themes which were evident at Mana; warmth and brilliant sunshine, languid power casually spread among myriad white beaches. A colony of Carmine Bee-eaters formed an ephemeral kaleidoscope of airborne tropical colour. There were black buffalo and white egrets, a squabble of baboons, shaggy waterbuck and skittish impala; all a dizzy sensory bombardment as we spun lazily along to the careless whims of chortling currents.

Hippopotami are gregarious animals and spend much of their daytime dozing half-submerged in shallows adjacent to deep-water channels. Although safari guides could recount many tales of 'rogue' animals attacking canoes, we had never experienced any problems. Outboard motors can be heard underwater long before they are seen, therefore we surmised that hippos were well warned of our approach and had already taken evasive action if they felt threatened.

Hippos hate to be cornered without a clear line of flight to deeper water. Now we approached a group of perhaps one hundred, and while reluctant to abandon our transect count, we were appreciative of their heightening anxiety. Mike activated the motor and held the dinghy stationary against the stream. We hoped the hippo would regroup and thereby open up a safe passage for us. Unfortunately, their confusion multiplied. Space was limited to a 40-metre channel between an island and the Zambian bank, its surface alive with snorting hippo that were popping up, lunging and crash-diving in ever-changing random patterns. We edged warily on, trying to maintain a 360-degree surveillance against possible attack. Suddenly the floor angled crazily as a hippo surfaced beneath us. We grasped for the stability of the rope railings while the boat lifted up and then slid sideways off the animal's broad shiny back. Both parties were taken by surprise and reacted with alacrity. He careened off with a monumental splash that enveloped me, and Mike gunned 'Skimmer' through the chaos to safety. Such is the dull humdrum of scientific research!

We settled in at Mwanja for a few days in order to write up our findings. Mwanja is situated at the entrance to the Mupata Gorge and, like Nyamuomba, is at a point of topographical transition. Unlike Mana the vegetation is predominantly *C. mopane* and the soils shallow and rocky. A thin line of lusher riverine woodland demarcates the watercourses. In the serene Mwanja evenings two rhino would pass near camp en route to water. It was a great thrill to quietly watch these rare bulky animals, so powerful and yet so vulnerable. We both felt a sense of pathos, as if watching a parade of creatures from epochs before, the doomed remnants of a forgotten age.

After restocking supplies and doing some maintenance work on

'Skimmer', we headed downstream and entered the beckoning Mupata Gorge. It is not as imposing as Kariba's, consisting of steep hillsides rather than true cliff faces, and the river does not hurry with quite the same urgency. However, the gentler terrain allows a greater variety of animals to enter its environs. We saw numerous groups of kudu, some secretive bushbuck, waterbuck, baboons, elephant, hippo and plenty of crocodiles. Almost immediately we found our old friends, the Rock Pratincoles. We stopped to investigate their rock islands and disturbed a Whitebacked Night Heron on her nest, deep within the recesses of a rock crevice. This is an uncommon bird and it was marvellous to see one so near at hand – and with three eggs into the bargain.

Scanning Mupata's hills we could appreciate that the varieties of trees colonizing these formidable slopes were quite different from those we encountered on the alluvial floodplain. Fay Robertson, a Parks botanist, was concerned about the escarpment vegetation. Assessment of aerial photographs taken over the last three decades shows significant reductions in the density of canopy trees. High rates of loss have occurred, about 20 per cent per annum of the previous year's total. The damage has been created by elephants. The loss rate of *Brachystegia* trees increased faster than the rise in elephant densities, which suggests that tree loss may have been accelerated after some threshold was passed. There are about 10 000 elephant in the Zambezi Valley Parks Estate, which averages out to approximately one elephant per square kilometre. Parks ecologists calculate that to maintain a canopy cover at acceptable levels (50 per cent) the elephant density has to be kept in the range of 0,1 to 0,5 per square kilometre.

Drought and fire can speed up the woodland destruction, but do not initiate it. Once an area of woodland is cleared, grasses become better established, and when dry, fuel a hotter fire. This in turn kills young saplings and prevents regrowth. Mature trees are remarkably resistant to fire, although certain species such as *Brachystegia glaucescens* are vulnerable. 'Early burning' has been practiced by Parks since 1978 in order to remove grass tinder while the bush is still relatively green from the rainy season. The burn is intended to create a patchwork of burnt and unburnt areas which achieves two objectives. The first is to prevent destructive late-season fires and the second is to encourage the maximum rate of regeneration which tends to occur in unburnt patches. Prevention of fire is ideal but impractical. In addition, the dead grass builds up with each fire-protected year until the tonnage of grass is twice what it would be if routinely exposed to fire. In these circumstances, fire is disastrous.

The Zimbabwe government maintains an elephant management policy. In other words, since 1965 they have culled elephants in order to preserve vegetation (*see* Concerns for the Future, p.170). However, consideration has

*The African Fish Eagle has longs claws and spicules on the pads of its feet for grasping fish. Usually the prey is caught 15 to 30 centimetres below the surface. Surprisingly the bird is able to fish in choppy, murky water.*

*It has been suggested that a dam should be built at Mupata Gorge to supplement Zimbabwe's limited hydro-electric power output. The ensuing lake would have a major impact on the unique Mana Pools area, a World Heritage Site.*

been given to a 'mixed policy'; that is, allocating elephants priority over trees in certain selected regions.

We drifted past the white markings painted on rocks by engineers to indicate the proposed site of the Mupata Dam. This dam would flood everything we had encountered downstream of Chirundu, including Rukomechi, Mana, Chikwenya, Chewore and Mwanja. That seemed an appalling price to pay for progress.

I noted a different primate species on the Zambian bank, the Samango monkey (*Cercopithecus mitis*), which had not been recorded on the Zim-

babwean side in this area. We wondered whether the river was a true limitation to its distribution, or was the district simply so remote that no-one had as yet collected a Zimbabwean specimen? Kevin Dunham once pointed out to us that museums are (quite rightly) very reluctant to accept anything other than a skin as evidence of a sighting. The case of the Sun squirrel (*Heliosciurus mutabilis*) supports that viewpoint. For some time people had been reporting unusual squirrels in the valley, definitely not the common arboreal squirrel *Paraxerus cepapi*. However, until one little fellow fell out of a tree and lay unconscious at the feet of scientists, it remained officially unrecognized.

At about 17h00 we rounded a bend and viewed our overnight destination, the Tunsa River. Waterbuck and impala were grazing on its small floodplain and numerous storks, geese and waders foraged at the water's edge. Opposite the Tunsa, on the Zambezi's Zambian bank, stretched an

unusually tall sand dune. We chose a particularly pleasant spot on which to camp; grassed alluvial terraces near an energetic mixed colony of Carmine and Whitefronted Bee-eaters. We cooked early, not wanting to start a fire at night in case we were shot as poachers by Parks patrols. Mike suspended our mosquito nets between two oars which we had secured vertically in the ground. Under our nets and safe from the attentions of nocturnal insects, we wriggled into our sleeping bags and dozed off. Mike woke up first. Never before had he heard such heavy breathing! Unable to pinpoint the origin – it was new moon and the night densely black – he nudged me. I sat bolt upright on awakening.

'What's that noise?!'

'Lion?' I ventured pessimistically.

We lifted the netting off our faces in order to see better into the murky darkness. The exhalations of air seemed to wash right over us. Simultaneously, we identified the source. Three metres away and blocking out the entire southern sky loomed the unmistakable silhouette of an adult black rhino. The immense square head and curved front horn pointed menacingly straight at us. It was like peering into the business end of a tank's gun barrel. Plainly we were the objects of the rhino's intense agitation, as he huffed and puffed, trying to ascertain our identity. Our camp was evidently right in the middle of his regular path. After an initial flood of relief that it was not a hunting lion, we realized our fate was still very much in the balance and certainly not in our hands. Rhinos never seem to do things in half measures: they wipe you off the face of the earth or flee in disarray. Mike assessed our options. Either we broke the world record for the sack race or we lay absolutely still. The choices were terrible, but with no refuge immediately near-

by, the latter option seemed more logical. By now the animal was, like us, in a state of high tension. It had never encountered mosquito nets before. The rhino executed a series of jumps and false starts, snorting all the while like a runaway steam engine. We fumbled with our zips, trying at least to get out of the sleeping bags. Abruptly the rhino whirled around, retreated five metres, squared on us again and then finally cantered away. At that, two others trotted past us and followed the first into the night. We dared to breathe again. Incredibly, Mike went straight back to sleep!

Several people had informed us of some hot springs on the Tunsa and we resolved to visit them. The Tunsa is a small brook in the dry season, but we saw a surprising variety of wading birds and antelope. The stream pebbles were coated white with sulphur, and perhaps it is the mineral-rich water that supports the lush grass and a prolific population of invertebrates. We walked on upstream, witnessing an unidentified goshawk snatch a bird from a flock of seed-eating Quelea. The water became warmer and soon we reached the source, a bubbling pool which was far too hot to touch. It was lined with brightly-coloured sediments of red and orange hue, and an earthy sulphurous odour permeated the locality. We lunched and then started on our return journey to camp, cautiously detouring around a lone bull elephant that was splashing about in the river.

The next day, after a pre-dawn start, we continued our river odyssey eastward, passing through a 'gate' in the hills and into inhabited farming areas until at last we reached the Luangwa-Zambezi junction.

A major Zambezi tributary, the Luangwa obtains its headwaters from the Mafinga Mountains of northern Zambia. Flowing consistently south-west, the river passes within a low-lying valley and receives significant input from the Lunsemfwa and Lukusashi rivers before joining the Zambezi as a broad muddy waterway. The Luangwa Valley contains two important game areas, the North and South Luangwa parks, both of which contain a tremendous variety of wild animals. Some species (such as giraffe) do not occur on the Middle Zambezi while others (puku, for example) are common in Luangwa and very rarely seen on the main river.

Norman Carr was a pioneer conservationist in these wilderness regions. Recently, several institutions have started working in the Luangwa Valley and are attempting to involve neighbouring villagers in game management and anti-poaching measures. Poaching, as elsewhere in Zambia, has severely depleted elephant and rhino numbers.

At its junction with the Luangwa River, the Zambezi forsakes both Zambia and Zimbabwe and flows onward into Mozambique. Here three

LEFT *Puku were first hunted in 1857 by David Livingstone. Although these antelope do occur on the Middle Zambezi, they are much more common in the Luangwa Valley where they utilize the narrow stretches of grassland which lie between watercourses and the woodland on adjacent higher ground. Puku have a tendency to associate with other species, especially impala* (RIGHT)*, which they will follow if the latter run off in panic.*

towns have developed; Luangwa in Zambia, Kanyemba in Zimbabwe and Zumbo in Mozambique. 'Skimmer' bobbed through the turbulence created by the mixing streams while both Mike and I peered downstream at the red rooftops of Zumbo. Unfortunately we were not permitted to venture further because of the anarchy created by Mozambique's civil war. It was tremendously alluring to look across into the forbidden territory. Reluctantly we turned back, motoring for two days against the current up to our Mwanja base. We did not feel defeated, as our expedition was simply destined for Mozambique on another day.

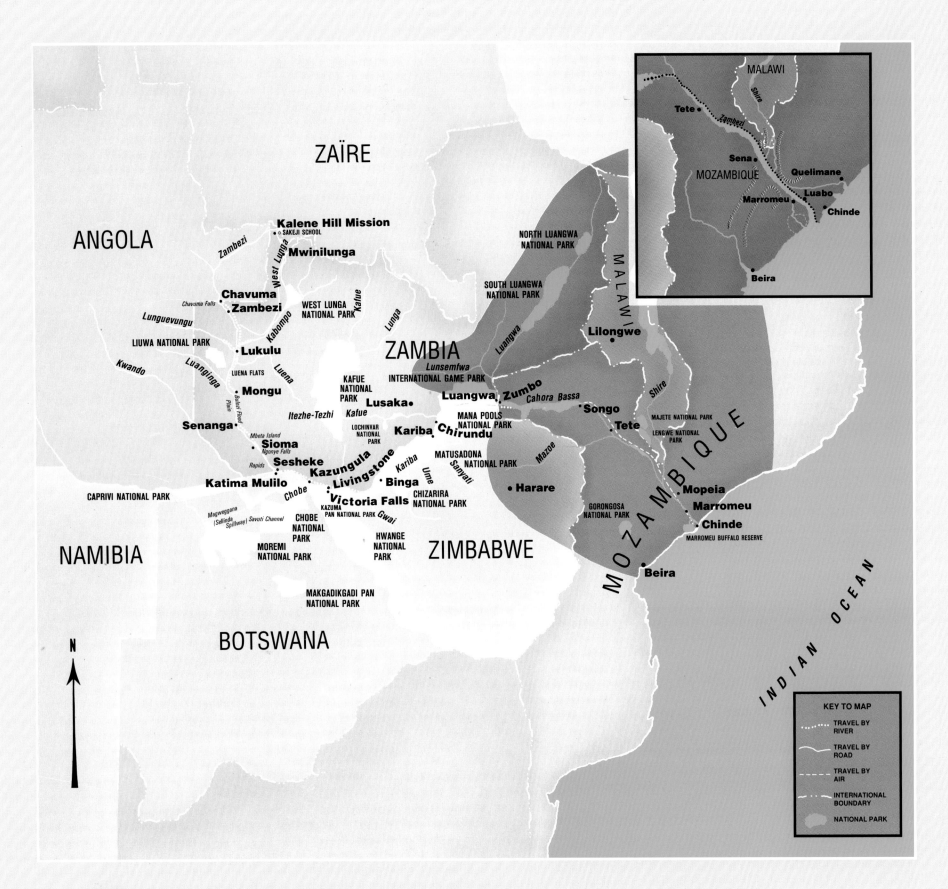

ZAÏRE

ANGOLA

NAMIBIA

BOTSWANA

ZIMBABWE

MOZAMBIQUE

ZAMBIA

MALAWI

INDIAN OCEAN

Kalene Hill Mission
○ SAKEJI SCHOOL
Mwinilunga
Zambezi
West Lunga
Chavuma
Chavuma Falls
Zambezi
Kafue
WEST LUNGA
NATIONAL PARK
Lunga
Lunguevungu
Kabompo
LIUWA NATIONAL PARK
Lukulu
Kwando
Luanginga
Luena
Luena FLATS
Mongu
Barotse Flood
Plain
Senanga
Mbeta Island
Sioma
Ngonye Falls
Itezhe-Tezhi
Rapids
Sesheke
Katima Mulilo
Chobe
Kazungula
Livingstone
Kariba
Magweggana
(Sellinda)  Savuti Channel
Spillway)
CHOBE
NATIONAL PARK
KAZUMA
PAN NATIONAL PARK
Gwai
MOREMI
NATIONAL PARK
HWANGE
NATIONAL PARK
MAKGADIKGADI PAN
NATIONAL PARK
CAPRIVI NATIONAL PARK

KAFUE
NATIONAL
PARK
Lusaka
LOCHINVAR
NATIONAL
PARK
Kafue
Kariba
Binga
Victoria Falls
Ume
CHIZARIRA
NATIONAL PARK
Sanyati
MATUSADONA
NATIONAL PARK
Mazoe
Harare

NORTH LUANGWA
NATIONAL PARK
SOUTH LUANGWA
NATIONAL PARK
Luangwa
Lunsemfwa
INTERNATIONAL GAME PARK
Luangwa
Zumbo
Cahora Bassa
MANA POOLS
NATIONAL PARK
Chirundu
Songo
Tete
MAJETE NATIONAL PARK
LENGWE NATIONAL
PARK
Shire
Lilongwe

GORONGOSA
NATIONAL PARK
Mopeia
Marromeu
Chinde
MARROMEU BUFFALO RESERVE
Beira

N

KEY TO MAP

TRAVEL BY
RIVER

TRAVEL BY
ROAD

TRAVEL BY
AIR

INTERNATIONAL
BOUNDARY

NATIONAL PARK

MALAWI
Tete
Shire
Zambezi
Sena
MOZAMBIQUE
Quelimane
Marromeu
Luabo
Chinde
Beira

140

# THE LOWER RIVER

*Expansive mangrove forests in the delta dissipate some of the fury of the flooding
Zambezi and thereby capture a portion of the river's alluvial load.*

# UNCHARTED WATERS

## CAHORA BASSA

*Jumbo Williams*

OUR LAND CRUISER WHINED in metallic protest when Mike engaged a lower gear. We were descending the legendary Alpha Trail, a sinuous north-easterly passage down Zimbabwe's Zambezi escarpment – a route which had, in the recent unsettled past, conveyed numerous troops to war. It was October and the Mavuradonna Range was unseasonably swathed in cloud. Occasionally the soft drizzle parted to reveal feathery Miombo canopies draped over the dripping hillsides in cascading exuberances of red and orange hue.

We reached the flat, expansive valley floor and found that the vegetation changed immediately to familiar broad-leafed woodland. Five bumpy hours later we arrived at the Zambezi. It had been two years since our last visit to Kanyemba. During that time there had been a number of important changes. Firstly, the security situation in Mozambique was more encouraging and consequently we had, after some perseverance, managed to obtain travel visas. Secondly, Mike was now married. Happily, his wife Joanne was able to join us for our proposed exploration of Cahora Bassa.

We completed immigration formalities at Kanyemba and drove into Mozambique, following the river eastward for some 20 kilometres along an old Portuguese road to our destination, Kafukudzi hunting camp.

The headwaters of Cahora Bassa reach Zumbo, a settlement founded on the Zambezi's north bank by the Portuguese in the 17th century. The vil-

lage is situated at the base of Madzvantsva Hill, the most prominent landmark of the region. H. de Laessoe passed this way in 1903 and thought the place 'completely decayed and ruined'. Present-day deprivations of civil war have done little to improve its lamentable state. Renamo rebels apparently controlled most of the lake's northern shoreline and consequently the government forces guarding Zumbo bore the brunt of hostilities. During these exchanges, the occupants of Kafukudzi camp could view the action from the safety of the government-held southern bank.

We established our base at Kafukudzi and managed, during our time on Cahora Bassa, to fly over the entire lake and also to boat downstream of Zumbo for approximately 100 kilometres. One of the first features to strike us was the turbid water. This is in strong contrast to the clear depths of Kariba and is the key to understanding the considerable differences between these two great Zambezi lakes.

Cahora Bassa is the fourth largest dam in Africa (after Lake Volta, Lake Nasser/Nubia, and Lake Kariba) and boasts a wall that is 138 metres high. It took from December 1974 till May 1975 to fill. The lake is distinctly divided into larger and smaller basins which have different characteristics depending on their depth and the exposure to prevailing winds. The belt of land between the high- and low-water level is relatively narrow along the northern shoreline, but very broad along the southern, gently shelving shoreline. More than half of the lake area remains shallower than 18 metres (mean lake depth) and so, on the south side, a one- to five-kilometre-wide drowned tree-line is present. The maximum inflow to Cahora Bassa is usually observed in March-April, some months after maximum rainfall in the catchment area. This pattern is also seen at Kariba, where the local rainfall causes a transient minor flood (termed Gumbura) which occurs earlier than the

---

LEFT *Mount Cone Negosi dominates the northern skyline of Cahora Bassa. The shoreline of the Messenguezi Basin is thick with dead trees. Woodland clearing was never undertaken on Cahora Bassa, just one example of the many contrasts with Kariba Dam.*

ABOVE *Colourful rock agama – sentinel of the granite gorge.*

subsequent major inundation (Murorwe) from the Upper Zambezi catchment area. Sometimes the two floods coincide, as occurred in 1916, 1934 and 1957 – with dramatic consequences.

Cahora Bassa is churned up during the period of strong south-easterly winds (April to September) causing deeper water layers to mix with those at the surface. The mixing depth extends well below 80 metres and implies that nearly the entire lake is intensively stirred to the bottom for at least five months of the year. This turbulence sweeps up bottom sediments and is responsible for Cahora Bassa's reduced water transparency. The lake water becomes heavily loaded with clay particles in concentrations compatible with those found in glacially-fed lakes and marine bays. Particle sizes are small and their sinking rates are exceedingly low. The suspended clay abundance is uniform across the lake and only significantly lower at the mouths of the principal rivers that enter the system. Deposition of the clay begins when the lake starts to stratify (September to October) and is also encouraged by the action of certain filter-feeding crustaceans (*Diaphanosoma* spp.).

The high clay load has a profound impact on the ecology of Cahora Bassa. Reduced water transparency means there is less light to stimulate photosynthesis. In addition, food substrates are bound to clay and thus less available to algae. These conditions result in a sparse pelagic phytoplankton community which, in turn, depresses the zooplankton population.

Zooplankton comprise the major food source for many commercial fish species – including kapenta. These fish feed most efficiently during those nights when the nearly full moon rises some time after sunset. During these hours zooplankton come near the surface and become suddenly vulnerable in the first light of the rising moon. Crustacean populations are decimated by the sardines and their numbers are thereby cyclically linked to the phases of the moon.

Zooplankton clearly face a survival dilemma. Filter-feeding species are more likely to find nutriment in the surface water layers but run an increased risk of kapenta predation. They solve the problem by migrating vertically, sinking during the day to hide at murky depths and ascending late at night to feed near the surface.

In 1975 Dale Kenmuir suggested that kapenta may colonize Cahora Bassa from Kariba and this was confirmed in 1982. However, at the time of writing, there has been no commercial exploitation of this resource, although we did meet some Zimbabweans who were planning to establish a commercial fishing enterprise near Songo. A number of peasant fisherfolk catch fish both for sustenance and to sell as merchandise. It has been calculated that the fish production (exclusively table fish) is only some 60 per cent of the total sustainable annual yield. If the estimated sustainable sardine yield of 8 000 tonnes is added to the table-fish resource, only about 29 per cent of the fish potential is currently being harvested. The species caught most commonly include tigerfish (*Hydrocynus vittatus*), *Labeo* spp. and chessa (*Distichodus schenga*). African lakes approach full exploitation at a critical density of about 1,5 fishermen per square kilometre; the density on Cahora Bassa is 0,45 fishermen per square kilometre. This low number is attributed to a variety of factors. First, the uncertain security – particularly on the north bank – makes a stable lifestyle exceedingly difficult. Second, gill nets are expensive and hard to obtain. A third problem became evident as we progressed down the lake. The prevailing winds have a long, unimpeded reach and generate a wicked chop of substantial amplitude which makes offshore navigation in dug-outs extremely dangerous.

We became acquainted with a small community of fishermen who were camping by the Chisabvu tributary. Their only supplies for a two-week stay were salt and mealie meal. Virtually their entire catch was sold directly to Zambian traders. Most of the business was done on a barter basis as the only store servicing the upper two-thirds of the lake was at Magoe, many kilometres away. The nets are suspended afloat by aquatic reeds. Fish caught are split longitudinally, cleaned and either smoke-dried or salted and then sun-dried. The latter method has the disadvantages of being slow and requiring a large salt supply. In addition, dermestid beetle infestation begins immediately during the drying process. However, it was the preferred method amongst the Portuguese and the tradition continues. The final product is

LEFT *Mozambican fishermen almost exclusively use dug-outs on Cahora Bassa. These craft are extremely hazardous in rough water and fishing activities are consequently curtailed in the lake's more open basins.*

ABOVE RIGHT *The ultimate concern of the Cahora Bassa fisherman is to convert his catch into material profit. Commercial markets are not readily available and usually the fish are bartered in exchange for clothing and mealie meal.*

OVERLEAF *Adult hippopotami can stay under water for five to six minutes at a time, the young for much shorter periods. On returning to the surface they empty their lungs with a loud blast which can be heard over a considerable distance and is a useful warning to boatmen.*

protected from rats by storing it on racks which stand in the shallows. At that time, the current price for one fish was $1,50 (Zimbabwe), 20 Kwacha (Zambia), or 1 500 Meticais (Mozambique).

The fishermen use dug-out canoes almost exclusively. The best trees available for the construction of these craft are Pod mahogany (*Afzelia quanzensis*) and Wild mango (*Cordyla africana*). Other species used include Sausage tree (*Kigelia africana*) and *Acacia albida*. Boatmen claim their craft have a working lifespan of about 20 years, although canoes made from *A. albida* last only about five. Paddles are made from *Ziziphus mauritiana* (the pods are made into kachaso – an alcoholic distillate) and White syringa (*Kirkia acuminata*). Many of these 'dug-out' trees are constituents of riverine forest, most of which (85 per cent) was drowned by the lake. The fishermen now utilize the trees found along tributaries, and construct the boat 'on site'. A major effort is often needed to transport the finished product to water and this is effected by rolling the canoe on logs.

At the top end of the lake there are a considerable number of villages, but as the lake widens, so habitation dwindles. Subsistence agriculture is practised but there are no cattle on account of the tsetse fly. The area between Magoe and Kanyemba encompasses two hunting concessions; the Messenguezi River demarcates their common border. We encountered very little game, but some impala, klipspringer, Sharpe's grysbok, bushbuck and kudu

ABOVE *This backwater pool near the Chisabvu River was diminishing daily through evaporation and the fish became concentrated in an ever smaller volume of water. Along with other species, Saddlebilled Storks gathered for the feast.*
OPPOSITE *Yellowbilled Storks rely on their sense of touch to gather food. They stride slowly through shallow water with the bill immersed and held slightly open, all the while stirring the bottom substrate with their feet to disturb prey – in this case catfish.*

were seen. Buffalo, eland, sable, zebra and elephant are present, but animals in hunting regions learn quickly and are wary of revealing themselves during daylight hours. Other residents include hyaena, leopard and lion.

A wildlife reconnaissance of the Cahora Bassa environs was executed in 1970, prior to construction of the dam. The investigators found the ungulate population was low and highly dispersed. This is in contrast to the prolific game areas a little further upstream. Reasons quoted included the dense occupation of alluvium by cultivating man which discouraged the game from utilizing the riverine vegetation as a dry-season food source and refuge. In addition, 'The area has been out of the way of any development or law enforcement so that it has been the long-time "private" hunting ground for all and sundry.' That position has not changed. Almost every day we heard the sound of gunfire, sometimes muzzle-loaders, sometimes automatic weapons. The Mozambique government issues AK-47 rifles to villagers so that they can defend themselves against the Renamo bandidos. It is perfectly understandable that the same weapons will be employed to supplement the not too well stocked larder.

Hunting concessions operate under trying circumstances. The logistics of pampering an international client in the war-ravaged bushveld of Mozambique are very difficult. Safaris can be lucrative – an elephant hunt (minimum of 15 days) costs over US $900 per day. In 1990 the Mozambique government stopped all elephant trophy hunting and the owners of the concessions had to rely on buffalo and cats for an income, but this is not nearly as remunerative. Unfortunately the ban has done nothing to improve the lot of the Mozambique elephant because the illegal carnage continues daily. All the government has done is discourage rational game management and deprive itself of a source of foreign currency.

There have been other forms of game exploitation in the area. Crocodile eggs are collected yearly (8 000 this last season) for the two crocodile farms situated in the Bazaruto Archipelago. In the recent past crocodile and hippo culls have been authorized. These populations were hardly monitored at all, so one can only speculate that the decisions to harvest were made empirically.

During our progression down Cahora Bassa, we were to find the lake dominated by a series of hills, all of which occur on the north bank. Madzvantsva towers 600 metres above the lake inlet. Here, the Zambezi tenaciously retains its riverine characteristics, flowing swiftly between streamlined sandy islands.

The surrounding countryside is wooded, with mopane growing on calcareous clays, *Terminalia sericea* on sand, *Kirkia* and *Commiphora* on stony soils and *Acacia tortilis* (among others) on alluvium. There are areas of floodplain grassland and the aquatic plants are dominated by *Phragmites mauritianus* and *Eichhornia crassipes* (Water hyacinth).

There was considerable concern, during construction of the dam, that an explosive growth of floating aquatic plants (macrophytes) would occur, as happened with *Salvinia molesta* on Kariba. This could interfere with hydroelectric installations and water transport, and affect fishing, navigation and recreation. Of the four possible species which could form weed mats (*E. crassipes*, *S. molesta*, *P. mauritianus* and *Pistia stratiotes*) Water hyacinth established complete dominance, but covered less than one per cent of the surface area. Its spread is limited by wave action and the large fluctuations in water level.

The bird life was typical of the Middle Zambezi. Again we encountered breeding African Skimmers. This is in contrast to Kariba, where suitable sandbanks do not occur and African Skimmers disappeared from the area after the lake filled.

There are other differences between the two lakes. Kariba is longer, wider and contains a greater water volume. Cahora Bassa has the greater maximum depth but is generally shallower. Kariba displaced 50 000 people, Cahora Bassa 7 000. There was no tree clearing on Cahora Bassa. The prevailing wind follows the long axis of the Mozambique lake more closely and has a

longer reach. Theoretically, it should be a more tempestuous body of water. Cahora Bassa discharges through its sluice gates and the water level fluctuates much more than at Kariba. At Kariba *S. molesta* is the predominant macrophyte. There is less game at Cahora Bassa and no game reserves, no tourist industry, no commercial fleet and no industrial development. Communications are virtually non-existent. It generates hardly any power.

On Cahora Bassa we used an inflatable dinghy with a substantial aluminium keel that conferred a 'V' shape to the hull and was thus suitable for rough lake conditions. We were delighted to be accompanied by two other men, Steve Edwards – a professional hunter – and Kingston, his tracker. During our progression down the lake we established three camps and spent a number of days at each, investigating the surrounds. The lake's shoreline is irregularly dotted in this section by makeshift grass huts which the fishermen use during their sojourns away from home. At any one time many of these shelters remain unoccupied and we settled in one at Chisabvu for our first camp. Daytime temperatures were reaching 45 °C, which made it imperative to have some midday shade. There were some fishermen about a kilometre upstream and we boated over to meet them. Our neighbours were heartwarmingly courteous and eager to help – a theme that was to be repeated many times over in Mozambique. It was a salutary lesson when one remembers the needy circumstances these people endure.

At Chisabvu the lake is some four to five kilometres wide but has a river-like character and a remarkably strong current. A feature of Chisabvu is the extensive backwaters, low-lying areas which become inundated during high water. It was the end of the dry season and many of the inlets were nothing but barren depressions of cracked mud, with dehydrated fronds of hyacinth festooned on the upper branches of once-submerged trees like the abandoned decorations of last year's Christmas party. A few pools remained and these contained a multitude of trapped fish. They were host to scenes of intensive avian activity, with pelicans, storks and herons systematically combing the shallows for a piscatorial prize.

Madziatenta was our next staging point, perhaps 60 kilometres beyond Zumbo. This seemed a major transition zone for Cahora Bassa because it was the first time that the Zambezi's current was not noticeable. Extensive

ABOVE *The Threebanded Plover makes up for its diminutive size by comprehensively combing the shoreline in an energetic and business-like manner. It moves in a series of short, rapid spurts, stopping abruptly to probe the mud vigorously.*
RIGHT *Ruff breed in northern Europe and Asia and then migrate to Africa, usually arriving in the Zambezi area in August. Females are termed Reeves and usually outnumber the males within the flock.*

drowned treelines were evident and we constantly encountered the rolling waves of open water. Signs of elephant were common and among some grass huts we found the discarded remains of sable, vervet monkey, civet and grysbok – all killed 'by wire' (snared).

Madziatenta means 'Hot Springs'. They were located on the north bank and arranged in clusters within a verdant growth of knee-high emerald grass.

The hill country of the north bank is formed by coal-bearing sedimentary strata abutting on granite. *Brachystegia* woodland is more common in this area as the rainfall is higher. We traced a stream back into the hillocks. Certainly, the bush appeared different from that of the lower-lying south bank and we seemed to encounter more birds. This is also Renamo country, so we did not stay overnight.

Our final destination was the Messenguezi River basin which is about 90 kilometres from the lake inlet. Here at last we found ourselves in a lacustrine environment which was at least superficially similar to that of Kariba. The water is turquoise and clearer, the bay expansive and the shore shallows densely packed with bleached mopanes. Mount Cone Negosi (1 145 metres) with its pyramidal shape, dominates the northern skyline. Camuenje Hill (then part of the mainland) forms an impressive south-bank cliff and leads

into a picturesque string of islands. We camped at the northern tip of this delightful archipelago. With the exception of the upper Messenguezi reaches, the hilly terrain was steeply sloped and only sparsely populated by fisherfolk.

Downstream of the Messenguezi-Zambezi confluence the lake is constricted to a width of one to two kilometres and forms a series of three 'narrows'. We motored through them to the Mucanha Basin which lies beyond and viewed the impressive flat-topped Mount Matemoe. This was the limit of our fuel reserves and, after a ceremonial swim, we had to turn back.

During our excursions on Cahora Bassa, we never encountered another motor boat – other than the two 'banana boats' at Kafukudzi camp. This was a rather unique situation and most enjoyable. We had no bandido problems and the only hitch came when our inflatable suddenly burst the seams of one of its compartments.

Joanne left us to return to civilization, while Mike and I prepared for the next stage of our venture – the Lower Zambezi. The flight to Songo was frustrating in that dense smoke blurred much of the view. However, Cahora Bassa Gorge was unmistakable. The terrain is immensely rugged and broken (quite unlike the flat horizons of Mosi oa Tunya) with granite peaks looming perpendicularly some 600 metres above the river. In contrast to Kariba, the double-curvature arched dam wall is placed about 10 kilometres within its gorge. It is impressive as an engineering spectacle. There are eight floodgates, with a total discharge capacity of 13 600 cubic metres per second. The turbines (four operational and one standby) can generate 2 075 megawatts of power. Another underground station is planned for the north bank with an installed capacity of 1 750 megawatts. The total output would be the biggest in Africa. Ironically, it probably has the least at present.

We landed at Songo town, a Portuguese-dominated enclave which is perched on a small plateau ringed by mountains. Hidroelectrica de Cahora Bassa (HCB) is the commercial enterprise charged with management of the dam complex and almost all of Songo belongs to HCB. After installing ourselves in the only hotel, we descended the road of 13 hairpin bends which transports workers down to the wall. The crests of distant blue-graded hills were laced with power lines. These aluminium-and-steel cables stretch as far as Pretoria in South Africa and are designed to transmit 533 kilovolts direct current, which has significantly less energy loss than alternating current. Renamo dissidents never damaged the generators, but have succeeded in totally disrupting the flow of electricity by regularly sabotaging the transmission cables.

Below the dam wall the Zambezi regroups in sullen fury. This is the 96-kilometre long, dreaded 'Kebrabassa'. The word means 'the work is done' and refers to paddlers of upstream-bound canoes, for whom the journey finished at the impenetrable gorge. Here Livingstone's 1858 expedition failed in its original purpose and the river remained undescended until H. de Laessoe's 1903 'journey of exploration' in two boats from the Gwaai River to the sea.

'... rugged granite mountains, towering 4 000 feet on either side of the narrow river, brought their boulder-strewn slopes right to the edge of the water. Our difficulties here increased enormously. The land passage became all but impossible ... Moreover, the heat of the sun in the narrow gorge is enormous, and we experienced the almost incredible fact that ... at midday the naked, black rocks become so heated, that they will blister your hands at the least touch.'

LEFT *The water level of Cahora Bassa fluctuates by as much as eight to 14 metres each year, and consequently large areas of the gently sloping southern bank are flooded during the peak season (March to May), only to become desiccated once more by November.*

ABOVE RIGHT *The drowned treelines in Cahora Bassa are a hazard to navigation and will pose difficulties for any commercial fishing industry.*

At one stage, De Laessoe's expedition exhausted their provisions.

'Being without food of any description, it became a question of covering as much ground as possible whilst we had the strength. Eventually, as no change occurred and the gorge seemed interminable, both we and the natives became reckless and negotiated rapids, and even falls, which, in sane moments, one would never have thought of attempting to descend.'

After three days of progressing in this manner, they reached the end of the gorge and met the overland members of their party. Kebrabassa was found to contain no less than 13 cataracts and 64 rapids.

We could only fly low over the gorge and it remains one of our chief regrets that the security situation prevented us from exploring this historic guardian of the secretive Zambezi. No doubt the dam has changed everything. From the air (always deceptive) the river looked navigable by raft, perhaps even by kayak. Once peace is restored, this will be a white-water experience comparable with the best.

# GATEWAY TO THE DARK CONTINENT

## CAHORA BASSA TO CHINDE

*Mike Coppinger*

AFTER TWENTY YEARS OF WAR, which continued to rage in 1990, the security and logistical problems confronting a traveller in Mozambique were considerable. Jumbo and I determined that we could most effectively gain access to the Lower Zambezi by chartering a light aircraft. Accordingly, we enlisted the services of Craig Saunders, a long-time Zimbabwean friend of Jumbo's. He was ideally suited to the assignment as he has an adventurous spirit with a colourful history of soldiering, travelling and hunting. Furthermore Craig is an exceptionally skilled bush pilot with extensive experience of flying in Mozambique.

The three of us spent a weekend in Songo under virtual 'hotel arrest' and were eager to get going on Monday morning. Craig was particularly restless – two days on the ground were enough for this aviator. We approached the airport administrator, a diminutive fellow named Paulino, to inform him that we were leaving for Tete as planned. He looked up calmly into Craig's face and said matter-of-factly, 'Good morning, I have a small message for you ... today Tete is closed.' That effectively meant that we were going nowhere. Craig towered over the little man and with incredulity and exasperation demanded an explanation of this small message. It was true – the Tete airport staff had recently decided that they were overworked and would therefore extend their weekends to include Monday.

The following day we were cleared to fly and while the sun was still low we were skimming the precipitous slopes of the dramatic Cahora Bassa

Gorge. The harsh, unrelenting terrain does not permit human habitation but as soon as the jealous rock walls allow the river some latitude, rough shacks can be detected on the gentler slopes.

An abundance of baobab trees and the thinning out of ground cover herald the proximity of Tete town. The commercial centre on the south bank is joined by a bridge to a more primitive, sprawling settlement clustered around rocky outcrops north of the river. Coming in to land, we detected the shapes of armoured tanks positioned around the perimeter of the airfield. After refuelling we pursued the Zambezi on its course through the predominantly flat, hot terrain of central Mozambique.

It was mid-October, a time when Africa burns. One can travel for thousands of kilometres and never be out of sight of fire: everywhere the tinder-dry countryside is put to the torch by local inhabitants. The result is an atmosphere thick with smoke and visibility is often restricted to less than 10 kilometres. Thus the vistas rolling beneath us lacked the sparkle they would acquire when the cleansing, life-giving December rains sweep across the sub-continent. Craig commented that the situation gets worse each year, particularly in Zimbabwe. He attributes this to rampant deforestation which compounds the problem by billowing ever more dust into the atmosphere.

Winding through the hills from the south came the wide sand bed of the Mazowe River, its shallow sheen of water a travesty of the torrent that surges into the Zambezi after good rains. The green flow of the main river was two kilometres wide and divided by a number of large islands. People have established their huts and crops on these spits of sand and reed in the hope that the water will offer some protection against the ravages of war.

The next notable feature lies between the hamlets of Sungo and Bandar. Here a range of hills trending north-south constrains the river briefly in the

LEFT *A bird which became an important element in our studies was the African Skimmer. As we boated in the river's mouth, it seemed touchingly appropriate that a flock of about a hundred strong should skim the Zambezi waters alongside us.* ABOVE *Fiddler crabs abound in the sticky alluvial mud of the delta.*

'S'-shaped Lupata Gorge. Downstream of this ridge a number of pans occur on the north bank, including Lake Danga, which in pre-Cahora Bassa days supported thousands of people on its fish. We were encouraged to note that there had been enough flooding, in spite of the dam, for the lake to still contain water in October and that a number of people in dug-outs were active on its surface. However, it is probable that the productivity of the lake has been greatly diminished.

A deceptive sign of development is a railway bridge spanning the four-kilometre-wide river bed at Sena. However, two steel sections of the defunct structure hang limply into the water. This forlorn reminder of Mozambique's woes over the past two decades is a legacy of the Rhodesian forces, who blew the bridge in the 1970s, thus dealing the region's economy a devastating blow.

Forty-five kilometres further on the Shire River, meandering languidly down from the north through a flat-bottomed valley, merges with the Zambezi. This confluence heralded our entry into an intriguing topographical arena. The basin occupied by Lake Malawi and the Shire is an arm of the Great African Rift Valley which stretches down the continent from the Red Sea. When the valley crosses the Zambezi it forms the Urema Trough which runs southwards for another 280 kilometres, capturing the flow of the Pungue River, before disappearing into the Mozambique Channel just south of Beira.

The Urema Trough is flanked by the Cheringoma Plateau to the east while the dominant feature on the western escarpment is Gorongosa Mountain. Gorongosa is typical of the cone-shaped inselbergs which characterize central Mozambique and play an important part in the region's ecology. High rainfall attracted to the mountain gives rise to perennial streams, the flow of which is a key to life in the surrounding midlands and adjacent Rift Valley. A similar function is performed by Morrumbala Mountain, situated some 20 kilometres north of the Zambezi-Shire confluence.

In times before the huge Kariba and Cahora Bassa dams the Zambezi floods used to overflow into the Rift Valley, pushing northwards up the Shire and south down the Urema Trough. In the exceptional deluge of 1958, when the mighty river defiantly swept aside man's first attempt to dam Kariba, the volume of water was so great that it swirled right through the Urema Trough and overflowed into the Pungue Basin. The power of those floods was illustrated by reports that the torrent had swept herds of buffalo and waterbuck off the delta plains and into the sea.

Leaving the Rift Valley behind and flying over the river town of Marromeu, we entered the Zambezi delta, a triangular area of 18 000 square kilometres with a sea frontage of 120 kilometres. The inland section of the delta fan is comprised mostly of grassland plains interspersed with swamps, streams and forest patches. The region is a natural haven for plains game, par-

ticularly buffalo and waterbuck. Ecologists estimate that the original buffalo population must have been in the vicinity of 130 000. In about 1938 organized hunting was started for skins and for meat to supply town settlement and the developing sugar industry. Buffalo, elephant, hippo, waterbuck, zebra and eland were exploited, with devastating effect.

The year 1960 saw the abolition of professional meat and ivory hunting, the introduction of safari hunting and constructive revision of conservation laws and law enforcement. These positive moves came too late for the plains north of the Zambezi, as they are now virtually denuded of wild animals. However, they did herald an era of fresh hope for the southern sector, which also benefited from the proclamation of the Marromeu Buffalo Reserve encompassing 1 600 square kilometres. In fact the game in the area recovered to the extent that cropping of buffalo on a sustainable yield basis was carried out between 1976 and 1982. Success in rehabilitating the area's wildlife was attributed largely to local people's involvement in the initiatives. Unfortunately, in consequence of the anarchy which has resulted from the escalation of civil war in the mid-1980s, the positive trend has been reversed, with animal numbers plummeting.

These plains owe their fertility to the rich alluvial soils deposited during centuries of annual flooding. In addition to providing nourishment, the regular inundation has protected the grasslands by keeping woodland encroachment at bay. Today the valuable silt settles in the depths of Kariba and Cahora Bassa and the life-giving floodwaters are regulated by the concrete barriers. Although the delta has on occasion been swamped since completion of the dams, inundation is now dependant primarily on the 'clean', or silt-free, run-off from the Cheringoma Plateau.

The big dams have also affected the fishing industry in the delta. The flood regime is a vital factor in the breeding cycle of many fish species, so it is obviously important that dam releases be managed to emulate the natural pattern as closely as possible. There is evidence that discharges from Cahora Bassa have been made with little consideration of the downstream implications. A dramatic example was the closure of the dam in December 1974: for two months, at a time when the river should have been flooding, its flow was reduced to less than 10 per cent of average. Fish which had already moved into marginal grasslands to spawn were stranded and died in vast numbers.

The government administrator at Chinde bemoaned to us that in recent years water has been released without his information; on such occasions the river people have suffered severely. In our discussions with older fisherfolk they consistently confirmed that their catches now are inferior to what they were on the free river.

About 40 kilometres from the sea, major distributaries start breaking away to the north and south of the main stream, cutting through a floodplain which is a mosaic of grass, reeds and palm trees. We followed the major channel, which heads in a south-easterly direction towards the coast. By the time we came within sight of the sea the vista beneath us had taken on the appearance of a bushy, olive-green cloak rent by a multitude of silvery sheets

*Below Cahora Bassa Gorge, the terrain surrounding the Zambezi becomes sufficiently hospitable to permit human habitation.*

*Early-morning mist imparts an ethereal quality to the Lower Zambezi. Sena Sugar's barge chugs upstream towards the town of Luabo (RIGHT) and later the vessel's military escort goes ashore in pursuit of armed rebels (ABOVE).*

of water. Closer inspection confirmed that we were soaring over an extensive canopy of tall mangrove forest.

Finally the river banks curl away from the channel and merge with the seashore, releasing the dark brown waters of the Zambezi to be swallowed by lines of gentle white surf rolling in from the Indian Ocean.

To the south lie two more vast estuary mouths, each marked by the stark hull of a ship trapped by shallow seas. A flat, sandy coastline bound by mangrove forests and cut by numerous smaller estuaries extends for 100 kilometres down to Beira. The uniformity of this wilderness of land and water makes distinction between the Zambezi and Pungue basins indiscernible.

We landed at Beira in a fierce crosswind, to be greeted by another 'small message': the news now was that the entire country had run out of aviation fuel. We were therefore hamstrung because our intention was to do extensive aerial reconnaissance of the delta. A positive development was that we made a rendezvous with Sansãu Bonito Mahanjane, an officer of the Wildlife Department (Direcção Nacional De Florestas e Fauna Bravia), who had travelled up from Maputo to accompany us on our exploration.

After a couple of days our host in Beira, Stewart Hogan, procured enough fuel for Craig to drop us off in the delta and return to Harare. We were dubious about the security situation on the ground but felt we had no option but to go ahead with this change in plan. So it was that late one afternoon we

winged our way over the enchanting plains of Marromeu. Flying low, we saw small groups of buffalo and several waterbuck as well as interesting sightings of zebra, bush pig and Wattled Crane. Bonito, head of Mozambique's anti-poaching unit, was particularly chagrined when we spotted a couple of probable poachers. He received some solace when we dive-bombed and forced them to lunge headlong into water for cover. Craig recounted how a year earlier he had been flying at low level in this area when a group of armed bandits emerged from the reeds and turned their weapons on the plane. In a reflex reaction our trusty pilot had dipped his nose and roared straight at them – sending bandidos scampering in all directions before a shot could be fired!

The sun was low in the west when the aircraft taxied to a halt in front of a tiny whitewashed building which passed as Chinde's airport. A balmy tropical atmosphere was accentuated by the warm wash of sunset colours behind a grove of coconut palms lining the grass airstrip. Within minutes we were surrounded by at least a hundred wide-eyed, excited African children. As Craig's aircraft climbed and disappeared in the fading light, we were keenly aware of our isolation in this foreign, war-torn country.

ABOVE *The Rio Chinde, a major Zambezi distributary, snakes across central Mozambique's coastal plain in an atmosphere clouded by dry-season bush fires.* OPPOSITE *A lone boatman returns home at day-break after a night of fishing off the Zambezi River mouth.*

It was dark by the time we had been allocated accommodation in the Director of Agriculture's house. We sat in a large living-room - bare except for a table, two chairs and a one-wheeled motorbike. A burning wick protruding from a diesel-filled beer can cast a flickering yellow light over the scene. In the shadows one could discern the scurrying forms of numerous baratas (cockroaches) and one popped loudly underfoot when I walked into the kitchen. There was no running water and the odour from the bathroom indicated plumbing problems. It would be 14 days before Craig returned!

Our apprehensions were soon put to rest as Bonito took charge and established a congenial atmosphere for us all. Our host, like most Mozambicans we met, showed us only friendliness and hospitality.

A small network of tarred roads, covering an area of one kilometre by 500 metres, delimits the extent of the commercial/residential centre of Chinde.

The few administrative buildings, houses and basic stores are all owned by either the government or the Sena Sugar Company. They are conventional European-styled brick structures – some of them quite grand in design – but all are desperately in need of a good clean and a coat of paint. Palm trees and white wind-blown sand encroaching on the wide streets and sidewalks give the town a relaxed, tropical air. A small generator supplies electricity to the little hospital and the residences of a few top officials. In the absence of any municipal water services, water is drawn from a number of wells located on individual premises.

The seafront and Zambezi channels constitute a water barrier which has effectively saved Chinde from bandit invasion. Thus it has become a refuge for displaced people from more vulnerable areas like Luabo, and a shanty-town has mushroomed around the 'commercial' centre. These dwellings are constructed in traditional fashion with reeds and palm fronds secured to a rudimentary framework of mangrove posts. Water is obtained from deep cone-shaped pits in the sand which expose shallow pools. The liquid is scooped up in coconut husks or tins affixed to long mangrove poles. Ironically, the lifestyle of the shanty dwellers seemed more appropriate and hygienic than that of the people in the brick-and-concrete shells in town.

This coastal settlement owes its existence to the navigability of the Rio Chinde, a major Zambezi distributary. Thus the port has developed as a staging point for river traffic. In previous centuries the trade would have been concerned primarily with slaves and ivory, while in the 1900s the river became a lifeline for the sugar industry. In 1907 the British-owned Sena Sugar Company was founded in Caia and then its headquarters were moved to Marromeu in 1910. The industry became the economic backbone of the Lower Zambezi region and an additional operation was initiated at Luabo in 1924. The two factories were supplied by sugar-cane plantations covering 25 000 hectares and by 1985 the company provided employment for 22 000 people. As sideline activities the organization maintained a cattle herd of 27 000 head and ran a coconut plantation in the delta producing copra.

Mississippi-style paddle-steamers, suitable because of their shallow draught, were used for all transport to and from the sugar factories until 1947 when Marromeu was linked by rail to Beira. When bandits destroyed the railway in 1983 the flow of traffic reverted to the river. The war terminated sugar production in 1985 and now a skeleton staff keeps the company alive by performing basic maintenance and administrative tasks. An occasional river service to Marromeu is still provided by the *Mezingo*, a paddle-steamer which has been plying the river since 1931, and a motorized barge.

At Chinde's harbour the estuary shoreline is littered with the rusting skeletons of craft ranging from large ocean-going vessels to lifeboat-sized tubs. Jumbo counted 70 hulls, which included one huge derelict ship anchored a little way offshore. We discovered that the dynamics of the estuarine coast have resulted in two previous Chinde towns falling prey to the ocean. These shipwrecks have now been positioned along the shore as protection against the erosive action of river and tide.

On our first morning in Chinde we followed a sandy path through the shanty-town. Emerging from the huts and palm trees we were greeted by an enchanting beach-front scene. Glistening mudflats extended seawards from the high-water mark for several hundred metres. Delicate sand patterns moulded by the receding tide were disturbed by a host of burrowing crabs pushing up tiny mud balls from their excavations. Across the whole expanse a multitude of waders darted about, busily probing the wet soil with their beaks in search of fresh morsels. The horizon, plumed with white surf, provided a backdrop to a number of distant Yellowbilled Storks and pelicans patrolling the water's edge.

Superimposed on all this natural activity, fishermen and their families pursued their daily tasks, governed largely by the rhythm of the tides. Dug-out canoes were silhouetted ethereally against the waves and men with nets slung over their bare shoulders strode across the flats. When the tide turned, some of them started seine-netting and children chased foam pushed along by the encroaching current. The advance of the ocean was quite visible, the water-line creeping forward a few centimetres every second.

Mangroves bordered the mudflats and extended up the sides of the Rio Chinde. We regularly employed the services of Andrei, a local boatman, to

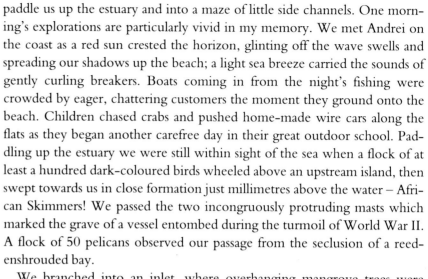

paddle us up the estuary and into a maze of little side channels. One morning's explorations are particularly vivid in my memory. We met Andrei on the coast as a red sun crested the horizon, glinting off the wave swells and spreading our shadows up the beach; a light sea breeze carried the sounds of gently curling breakers. Boats coming in from the night's fishing were crowded by eager, chattering customers the moment they ground onto the beach. Children chased crabs and pushed home-made wire cars along the flats as they began another carefree day in their great outdoor school. Paddling up the estuary we were still within sight of the sea when a flock of at least a hundred dark-coloured birds wheeled above an upstream island, then swept towards us in close formation just millimetres above the water – African Skimmers! We passed the two incongruously protruding masts which marked the grave of a vessel entombed during the turmoil of World War II. A flock of 50 pelicans observed our passage from the seclusion of a reed-enshrouded bay.

We branched into an inlet, where overhanging mangrove trees were vaguely reminiscent of the Upper Zambezi's Waterberry. We encountered one old friend, the Greenbacked Heron, who gave his familiar croak and flew off from a waterside perch. A loud, staccato call which repeatedly rang through the trees emanated from a Mangrove Kingfisher, a bird which is generally uncommon but ubiquitous here. The dazzling blue and red tones of both Mangrove and Malachite kingfishers frequently sparkled within the dark green foliage. The ebbing tide exposed sloping banks of black, slippery mud, which had its own specialized population. Fiddler crabs (*Uca* spp.) impressed each other with elaborate waves of their lopsided, enlarged pincers. Jumbo pointed out to a disbelieving Bonito how a fish could climb trees. This was the little mudskipper (*Periopthalmus cantonensis*) which skipped along the mud on its pectoral fins and was prone to hop up tree trunks.

The mangroves, in addition to providing a unique home for various life forms, play a vital role in the coastal ecology. Sandy coasts like this, unlike rocky shorelines, are very susceptible to erosion by wind and waves and depend on plant material to bind and stabilize the soil. The vast mud substrates of the Zambezi Delta are held in place by the mangroves. These extensive forests are also important in sustaining the large prawn populations on the Central Coast of Mozambique.

The Zambezi is one of a number of rivers that deposit heavy alluvial loads into the Bight of Sofala, which is a concave curve in the Mozambique coastline extending from Pebane in the north to the Save River in the south. The sedimentary build-up over the centuries has caused subsidence of the earth's crust, resulting in the inundation of the coastline and creation of a continental shelf up to 145 kilometres wide. An effect of this broad ledge of shallow sea is one of the highest tidal ranges anywhere on the African coast. Other

*Seine netting is a technique used by fishermen living along the delta beachfront. Their activities are governed by the tide as they exploit the waters of both the Zambezi channels and the Indian Ocean.*

characteristics of the bight, resulting from the heavy silt load, are the turbid waters and absence of coral. During the wet season muddy waters from the Zambezi discolour the ocean, but even at other times of year wind action has a tendency to stir up sediment from the shallow sea bed.

The alluvial loads are important for their provision of beach building material. Longshore drift distributes the alluvium along the beaches of central Mozambique, thus counteracting erosive wave action. Along the coast between Chinde and Beira we frequently observed clumps of mangrove stumps on the beaches, which is a sign that beach erosion is taking place and the sea is eating into the mangrove forests. This phenomenon has been apparent for several years and although it has not been studied in detail, it is probable that Kariba and Cahora Bassa have curtailed silt flow sufficiently to cause a deficiency of material needed to maintain the beaches.

Studying the fascinating intricacies of the delta ecology, we were surprised by two apparent absentees from the area. One was the Zambezi shark (*Carcharhinus leucas*). This feared predator of the south-east African coast is reputed to breed in the estuary and to travel long distances up the river whose name it bears. We repeatedly questioned the locals about its presence but the fish was apparently unknown to them. The other mystery surrounded the dugong (*Dugong dugong*), the creature which gave rise to the mermaid myth. This mammal has breasts similar to those of a human, but there the allusion to feminine enchantment ends. The huge, blubbery animal inhabits shallow coasts, grazing sea plants and algae and attaining a weight of up to 240 kilograms. Displaying a photograph of one to fishermen aroused no glimmer of recognition and our aerial searches were fruitless. On this evidence it appears that the dugong is not present in the delta, although it does still occur elsewhere in Mozambique seas, notably in the clear waters around the Bazaruto Archipelago.

After many false starts, we managed to secure a passage on one of the infrequent barge trips up to Marromeu. We joined about 50 other passengers on board early one beautiful moonlit evening. Bonito was not confident on water and when we lay down on the flat deck to sleep he was very apprehensive of the danger of rolling overboard, commenting balefully that we were now 'joking with our lives'!

ABOVE LEFT *The sticky black mud of the Zambezi delta nurtures extensive mangrove forests, which support their own specialized fauna. The fiddler crab has a lopsided appearance because of its one enlarged pincer.*

ABOVE *The mud skipper is a fish remarkable for the fact that it spends a good deal of time out of the water. It propels itself with brisk flicks of its tail.*

Our sleep was fitful as we lay fully clothed on the unsheltered, metal deck. At 23h00 the barge chugged into midstream to begin the journey. Our exuberant military escort – a handful of Frelimo soldiers – made their presence felt by strutting around the perimeter of the deck blowing whistles! The barge tied up for a few hours when the moon went down in the cold, damp hours of the early morning, but the motors growled into life again at 04h30.

Sunrise was muted by a blanket of heavy mist which limited visibility to a few metres. Trees materialized ghost-like out of the vapour and on one occasion we ran aground. Gradually the shrouds evaporated and we seated ourselves on the hold which was raised 20 cm above the deck and ran the length

of the barge in front of the wheelhouse. Once settled we got to work counting birds and noting the riverside habitat.

There was a large flock of Openbilled Storks on a sandbank off our port side which we estimated at 200.

'Ping, ping ... pop, pop ... pop, pop, pop ... pop, pop ...' - I dived onto the deck, taking cover behind the hold, as bullets whistled off metal. The shooting was coming from the north bank, some 150 metres distant. Pressing my cheek into the metal deck I noticed the alarmed Openbills taking to the air in a flurry of flapping wings. An Adidas kit bag and sundry items of luggage bobbed downstream after being dislodged by scattering passengers. Shouts of surprise and panic gave way to the more reassuring clatter of our troops returning fire at the unseen attackers. Given my naturally slim frame and the eagerness with which I attempted to mould myself into the barge, the raised hold afforded good protection. However, I reckoned without our helmsman's well-developed instinct for self-preservation: he had abandoned the wheel at the first shot. To everybody's great consternation the craft circled out of control, thus exposing our side of the boat directly to the gunfire.

Distressed by this turn of events I scampered to the back of the cargo section, en route to the other side of the boat. Great minds think alike, and so do terrified ones – I found Jumbo already there. We spotted a narrow opening in the metal sheets covering the hold and after a brief debate decided that was our best refuge on this merry-go-round. The intrepid adventurers hastily slithered through the gap and tumbled onto a pile of mealie meal bags in the gloom below. Our move did not go unnoticed and bodies were soon popping through the entrance like sacks off a conveyor belt. Having an aversion to confined spaces at the best of times my morale was not raised by Jumbo's comment, 'If they use rockets we've got a problem down here!'

Peeping through a small skylight I saw Bonito's wide eyes peering round a bundle of baggage. He soon joined the avalanche into the hold and his relief when he spotted us was obvious. He said afterwards, 'What would I tell my government if harm should come to you foreigners, for whom I am responsible? It would be better that I should be killed and you remain safe.'

After about eight minutes somebody took the wheel and steered the barge out of danger. Once everybody had recovered their composure we were told to remain below as the boat headed back to the scene of the attack. After off-loading the troops to do a sweep through the area we then backed off and waited on an island. When we went to retrieve our warriors Bonito shouted with pride, 'Look – they have trophies!'. One of the men was holding aloft the spoils of war – a green wooden table! Our fellow passengers roared their approval, while we collapsed with laughter. In the final analysis no casualties had been sustained by either side, a certain amount of baggage and one weapon had been lost overboard and one passenger had fallen into the river but had managed to clamber back onto the circling boat. Now with a carnival atmosphere prevailing we continued our passage in what had developed into scorchingly hot weather. There was no shade on the boat and no ablution facility.

When we docked at Luabo, Jumbo and I huddled under a disused fuel tank to get some shelter from the burning sun. The respite was particularly welcome to me as I was weakened by an upset stomach. In the distance we could see the ruins of the sugar factory. The town had been overrun by Renamo and occupied by them from July 1985 to March 1987. During that time they completely destroyed the infrastructure, wrecking the factory and town buildings and burning 143 tractors. The sugar operation is now totally incapacitated and will have to be revived from scratch.

As evening colours seeped across the sky from the upstream horizon we came within sight of the imposing silhouette of the Marromeu factory on the southern bank. By now I felt completely drained. We had endured a long, cold night, more significantly a long, hot day, had drunk little water, eaten one bread roll each and been shot at by bandits who had caused us to grovel on the deck and become absolutely filthy. Added to this, my stomach was

*Seen from the air, the Zambezi delta is a world of meandering waterways, forests, grassland and beaches.*

generating urgent distress signals as we approached the throngs of people crowding the rudimentary dock at Marromeu. They must have been amazed at my sense of purpose as I leapt ashore before the barge was quite stationary, pushed my way through them and disappeared into a maze of derelict railway carriages. I emerged some minutes later feeling a little easier and helped load our kit onto a Land Rover which Bonito had somehow managed to commandeer.

Marromeu town was depressing. War-damaged buildings littered the unlit, almost deserted streets and we did not relish the thought of the kind of accommodation we were likely to find. We failed to understand Bonito's discussions with the locals and our surprise was complete when the vehicle halted outside a building which actually had electricity. Wide-eyed, we were ushered into a well-kept house and shown a bedroom each, two impeccably clean bathrooms with flush toilets, a dining-room and a lounge. We were in a Sena Sugar Estates guest house. Seldom have I been so appreciative of a bit of comfort – after being served a dinner of chicken and chips I ended this day of extremes by climbing between a pair of crisp, cool sheets and collapsing into deep, restful sleep.

The General Director of Sena Sugar in Marromeu was a gracious man who was happy to show us around the sugar operation. After training in Portugal and Cuba he came to Marromeu in 1980, and since then he has witnessed the demise of the factory: once it was the third most productive in Africa; now it is a barren shell. The turning point came on a rainy day in January 1986. Using the wet, overcast conditions to maximum advantage two columns of Renamo rebels advanced undetected through the sector lying adjacent to the upstream river. Achieving total surprise they burst into town in a torrent of gunfire, routing the 1 000-strong Frelimo garrison. The Director and a few others managed to escape the onslaught, fleeing across country on foot to Chinde. The carnage of the occupation was great, the invaders reportedly having to use bulldozers to clear bodies off the streets.

The bandits then set about ransacking the town. The bank was blown up and robbed, the factory generators destroyed, and the warehouse of processed sugar looted. However, the destruction was on a much smaller scale than was the case at Luabo because the occupation was cut short. Fourteen days after the invasion a helicopter-borne Zimbabwean force landed south of the town and after two days of fierce fighting restored the status quo. Nonetheless, the damage had been done – the factory was incapacitated and thus Marromeu's back was broken. The cattle herd has been devastated and now only 500 head roam the estate. The work force has been reduced to a skeleton staff of 2 000 doing basic maintenance of the factory and fields. However, the Director lives with the hope that Marromeu will regain its former eminence. Plans are already afoot to rehabilitate the factory, and the cogs could start turning again within two years if a meaningful degree of security can be attained. In anticipation of this eventuality a small sugar crop was planted in March 1990.

In bidding us farewell the Director hospitably said we would be welcome

back at any time, but added philosophically that in times like these he could not guarantee that he would still be there on our return. We felt the town was secure and reckoned that his fears were unfounded. At midday the comforting vision of Craig's Cessna materialized out of smoke-smudged skies and dropped towards us. On greeting him we discovered that he had looked for us at Chinde before learning that we had travelled upstream. We told him of our adventures on the river and he responded cheerily, 'Oh! Well, I've just had a little squirt from below as well – also in the vicinity of Luabo!' He had been flying along the river at fairly low level when he heard the heart-stopping 'crack, crack, crack' of bullets splitting the air close to his cockpit. Banking abruptly and then climbing, he managed to escape without sustaining any damage. After swapping war stories we lifted off into the hazy heavens at 14h30. The next day we heard that bandits made a hit-and-run attack on the town the same afternoon. We reconsidered the Director's parting words.

Flying over the buffalo reserve en route back to Chinde the panorama of the great plains was obscured by bushfire smoke. A blaze was burning along a north-south transect, throwing up a tall, grey curtain from horizon to horizon. When we crossed east of the line there was a dramatic change of scene as we entered skies which had been kept clear by the prevailing sea breeze. An incongruous touch was added when the sinister forms of two huge Russian helicopter gunships loomed out of the smoke. Craig confided that in the past he had seen these aircraft land at Quelimane piled to the roof with waterbuck carcasses.

Spending one last night in Chinde we said our goodbyes, then in the early morning traced the coast down to Beira. Conditions were idyllic. The sea was flat and unusually blue with only the immediate vicinity of the estuary mouths discoloured by mud. Tiny specks on the ocean two kilometres offshore proved to be precariously floating dug-out canoes. These craft are a characteristic feature of the river from its earliest navigable point, and their presence on the open sea symbolized the extent to which the great river's influence extends far beyond its banks.

The receding mouth of the Rio Zambeze prompted a moment's reflection. We considered the fresh liquid which even now would be bubbling around that giant evergreen tree so far away in the interior of the continent. On their journey those waters would adopt moods varying from gentleness to vicious ferocity; they would compose scenes of rugged confinement alternating with open freedom; they would nurture new life whilst witnessing the ruthless finality of predation. They would express the wonder of God's creation with rare and priceless eloquence. We were deeply thankful for the privilege of sharing so many intimate moments with this giant of African rivers.

---

*Distributaries of the Zambezi fan out through the flat alluvial plains to span a 120-kilometre coastal front. A high tidal range has resulted in the formation of wide, gently sloping beaches.*

169

# CONCERNS FOR THE FUTURE

## Jumbo Williams

We believe that the future of the Zambezi is an international and public issue and that dissemination of information is therefore vital. This chapter is an overview of the factors Mike and I consider relevant to the Zambezi's future.

In the last decade, the Zambezi has become more accessible to both the developer and tourist because peace returned to the middle third of its course. As a result local and international interest focused once again on this secluded river. Foreign aid became available and the United Nations designated the basin a priority region for development.

Possibly the biggest asset that the Zambezi has is its unspoiled natural beauty. The near-pristine wilderness areas along the Zambezi support a diverse and rich biota. The fundamental ecological principle that all components of ecosystems are interrelated and that species do not live in isolation is nowhere more true than along the Zambezi. It is therefore our responsibility to ensure the survival of indigenous species of fauna and flora in viable populations, so that genetic diversity is not compromised and thus remains available for the benefit of future generations of mankind.

## BACKGROUND ISSUES

### International boundaries

Eight countries have borders within the Zambezi drainage basin and not all of these have been, or are, politically aligned. Communications are sometimes deficient and administrative decisions are taken without considering all the parties involved. (One extreme example: in 1978 Zimbabwe neglected to inform Cahora Bassa that four Kariba sluice gates had been opened and thus created an emergency situation as far as the downstream dam was concerned.)

Poachers have benefited enormously from the protection the borders afford. For instance, poachers operating out of Zambia have plundered Zimbabwe's black rhinos in the Zambezi valley.

### War

All of the Zambezi nations have experienced military violence of some sort in the last decade. Civil war continues in Angola and Mozambique, affecting at least 35 per cent of the river's course. Conflict stops economic growth and development. It discourages tourism, provides firearms for poaching (troops need food), disrupts communications and transport, kills game (landmines are exploded by elephants) and interferes with the implementation of an effective conservation policy. Usually the rural population starves and has to rely on the bush for food.

### Socio-economics

Zambezi countries have limited economies and the national budget for conservation is usually small; there are other priorities (health, education, military spending). Demand for land and food is escalating because population increases are among the world's highest. Political considerations play a role, as promises made during the heady days of the liberation struggle are remembered. Generally, there is a lack of basic infrastructure and a paucity of equipment and trained personnel. Corruption is not uncommon and bureaucracy tends to stifle initiative. There is a lack of education in, and public awareness of, conservation matters. In addition, conservation priorities differ from those of the developed world. For example: erosion, fire damage, overgrazing and deforestation are perennial African problems.

### Tsetse fly

The tsetse fly is often described as the guardian of African game – a generalization which is not always true. There are two common species of 'fly' along the Zambezi, *Glossina morsitans* and *G. pallidipes*. They are vectors for *Trypanosoma rhodesiense* and *T. gambiense* – the causative organisms of human sleeping sickness – and *T. brucei*, which is responsible for nagana in animals. Very few people along the Zambezi contract the disease as only about one per cent of the flies are infected and ungulates are by far the preferred hosts. Sleeping sickness is often fatal if untreated and nagana remains so uniformly lethal to cattle that pastoralists have had great difficulty in penetrating the 'fly belt'. Cattle can exist in fly country if given Samorin prophylaxis, but this drug is not benign.

Attempts to eradicate the tsetse fly have consistently had significant repercussions for Zimbabwe's wildlife, as the methods used have included mass game eradication and the creation of 'game-free' corridors. Insecticides have now superseded these.

Initially, ground spraying was done with dieldrin but DDT soon became the pesticide of choice and is applied to tsetse refuge, resting and breeding sites. Some experimental spraying has been done using deltamethrin, employing doses said to be considerably in excess of the

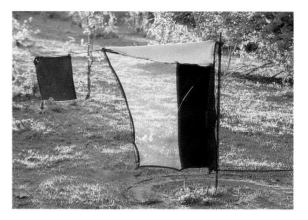

*A tsetse target. Flies, attracted to these devices by a combination of movement, colour and odour, die after contact with an insecticide-impregnated screen.*

recommendations of researchers who worked with the substance elsewhere in Africa.

Aerial spraying was initiated in 1957 using BHC, and endosulfan was first utilized in 1974 at Gokwe. Zimbabwe, Zambia, Malawi and Mozambique appealed to the European Economic Community (EEC) for assistance in regionally eradicating the fly and in 1986 the EEC commenced a three-year investigative phase to assess the feasibility of the project. Endosulfan was applied by aerial spraying and about $20 million was spent in the first phase. Subsequent sampling has shown that tsetse flies returned in substantial numbers to some treated areas, though there is debate as to whether these are 'survivors' or 'invaders'. It has been recommended to EEC management that a further investigative period is required to study spraying in hilly terrain (perhaps from helicopters) and to find an answer to the invader/survivor dilemma. Fortunately, tsetse flies are unusually sensitive to endosulfan and low doses can be used; sometimes deltamethrin is added. The EEC intensively monitored the environment for untoward effects and did not discover any significant problems, although admittedly they looked at families rather than individual species. Fish and aquatic life are at risk and do die if exposed to an overdose. Unlike DDT, endosulfan is unlikely to accumulate as it is rapidly detoxified once taken up by organisms.

Tsetse 'targets' were developed in Zimbabwe and have proven to be a cheap and effective way of controlling the fly. As they have minimal pollution potential, the devices are an attractive alternative to spraying and further work is underway to ascertain the most efficient spacing pattern. Economists advise that the targets should be able to last a year without maintenance because the main cost is road and vehicle upkeep.

Experts involved in the EEC project believe that eradication will take several decades. Some people consider eradication an inappropriate goal as war-torn Mozambique will continue to constitute a potential focus for re-infestation. In addition, there are conservation implications in eliminating an organism from National Parks estates.

## What are the qualities of the Zambezi?

The Zambezi is a large and energetic body of flowing water. It also has a wealth of indigenous fauna and flora which have aesthetic, educational and economic value, as well as providing a reservoir of genetic diversity for the future.

The river's resources are currently being utilized in several ways:

Industrially, the Zambezi is not over-utilized (the first large-scale factory we encountered was only 100 kilometres from the Indian Ocean!). Some heavy industry is present. There are three hydro-electricity schemes. Coal is mined in the Middle Zambezi. Oil prospecting was undertaken in Luangwa and a large network of roads hacked through the bush to accommodate the seismographic machinery. When operations moved to Zimbabwe, conservationists opposed the methods used and an acceptable compromise was eventually achieved.

However, the Zambezi is mainly exploited for its natural heritage. This embraces such diverse activities as tourism, game management, fishing (commercial, sport, and subsistence), prawn aquaculture, commercial farming (sugar, cattle, rice and coconuts), subsistence farming and water transportation.

Tourism is still in its infancy along much of the Zambezi and has – in our opinion – been badly neglected as a revenue source.

The term 'game management' is used in its widest sense to include community development projects, crocodile ranching, sport and commercial hunting, adventure and camera safaris, livestock capture and breeding, and meat and skin production. These practices are pragmatically attractive to developing nations. For wildlife to survive, it must be able to pay its own way, or how else can governments justify expenditure on conservation when the human population is semi-literate and starving?

Aid schemes have increased in the last decade and were present from the source (fish farming) to the delta (rice plantations). Foreign aid is useful, but unfortunately assistance usually comes late, when a situation has significantly deteriorated. Remedies are consequently often hurried and valuable only in the short term. Many schemes ultimately fail, perhaps because they were imposed upon the local people, who thereby do not identify with the objectives.

Frequently aid schemes involve land usage and yet we often found the ecological impact of a project was forgotten. Agricultural development through aid is occurring on the Barotse floodplain and Mozambican delta. Both these ecosystems are highly complex and if inappropriately manipulated may be severely damaged.

## CONCERNS

### Expedient development and unplanned settlement

How do the governments of Zambia and Zimbabwe plan to exploit the Middle Zambezi once the tsetse fly has gone? This question is central to the region's future. Development of the river is sometimes undertaken without appropriate investigation into the ecological ramifications, or the recommendations made after such investigations are simply ignored. The economic consequences of this unbalanced attitude are ultimately high. Development should be controlled, regionally coordinated and subject to an overall planning strategy.

The Middle Zambezi valley is a semi-arid environment with infertile soils. Virtually all of the Zambezi shoreline within Zimbabwe is designated as either Wildlife Area or Communal Land. The communal lands within the valley are generally unsuitable for conventional subsistence agriculture or intensive cattle grazing. In some places the sheer weight of human numbers has destroyed most indigenous resources, including wildlife and its habitats. But even in less densely settled areas, where natural ecosystems were able to survive, protectionist legislation prohibited their economic exploitation. They were often replaced by cultivation and cattle (tsetse flies permitting) – again to the detriment of the environment. Wild animals came to be perceived as little more than pests, liable to cause damage to crops or injury to cattle and humans. Apart from trypanosomiasis, other livestock problems occur. Foot-and-mouth is a disease endemic among buffalo which, like nagana, does not greatly affect indigenous game. The EEC buys Africa's beef on a preferential basis, provided the national herd is free of foot-and-mouth. In order to establish a commercially viable cattle herd alongside the Zambezi it would be necessary to exterminate the buffalo or rid its population of foot-and-mouth – both daunting options.

It is widely recognized that indigenous wildlife is one of Africa's greatest natural assets and can be used by rural communities to generate income and improve the quality of their lives. These benefits may encourage people to change their attitudes towards wildlife, help ensure the survival of natural ecosystems and thus reduce the environmental degradation that results from rural poverty. Zimbabwe's Communal Areas Management Programme for Indigenous Resources (Campfire) project evolved from this concept. Campfire is a philosophy of sustainable rural development that enables communities to manage and benefit from indigenous wildlife. It is essentially an entrepreneurial approach, based on game management.

Campfire depends on several interlinked ecological, economic, legal, social and institutional factors. Ecologically, it hinges on the proposition that indigenous wildlife is likely to be the most appropriate form of land use in areas of marginal agricultural potential. Economically, it requires the existence of markets for the 'goods and services' that wildlife can provide. It is also important that returns accrued should compare favourably with those generated from other forms of land use. A legal framework is necessary to enable the system to function and problems such as the ownership of wildlife must be addressed. The crux of the Campfire concept is that it cannot be imposed from outside. Projects must evolve from informed decisions taken by rural communities themselves. All game belongs to the state. However, the 1975 Parks and Wildlife Act (Zimbabwe) gives appropriate authority to responsible councils to receive and distribute the proceeds from wildlife

*Deforestation, erosion and overgrazing are evident in parts of the Middle Zambezi Valley. Unplanned settlement further aggravates these problems.*

management without passing them through Treasury.

By the end of 1989, 11 district councils had formed wildlife management bodies and nine other areas were identified as being potential Campfire projects. The progress to date is encouraging and is documented in several publications (see References).

There are similar projects elsewhere on the Zambezi (for example in the Luangwa Valley) which attempt to reconcile the interests of both development and conservation. All these schemes take many years to become adequately established and evaluated. Unfortunately the processes that prompted their initiation march on with inexorable haste. Unplanned settlement, and its consequent environmental degradation, has already occurred in the Zambezi valley. It is vitally important that Zambezi countries identify their long-term goals and do not allow non-sustainable or inappropriate development to gain a foothold.

### Poaching

Zimbabwe, unlike Zambia or Mozambique, has a 'shoot on sight' policy against poachers. Until recently the commercial poaching onslaught in the Middle Zambezi was directed primarily at the black rhino. Now more elephants are being slayed, a sure indication of the extent to which rhino numbers have declined. Estimates of the world's black rhino populations show an unmistakable trend. In 1960 there were thought to be 100 000 rhino, but only 68 000 in 1970, 15 000 in

Zimbabwe's war of liberation ended more than a decade ago, yet uncleared minefields still claim the lives of elephants.

1980, and perhaps 3 000 in 1990. About 60 per cent of Africa's black rhino live within the Zambezi basin, making it a vital region to conserve.

In North Yemen rhino horns are used for the elaborately decorated handles of ceremonial daggers. Fortunately, the importation of horn is now prohibited and with luck, as the tradition declines, so will the demand.

However, there is another market, in the Far East, which shows no evidence of abating. Horn is prized as a panacea, especially for fevers, and as an aphrodisiac (I worked with one Chinese cardiac surgeon who was adamant about its antipyretic properties). One male black rhino may carry three to four kilograms of horn. The final consumer price is about US $20 000 to 30 000 per kilogram. Taiwan has become the main Asian import centre as the Taipei government is not enforcing its own 1985 ban on the trade of rhino horn.

Of course, the poacher receives only a tiny fraction of the retail value but it is still a tremendous amount of money in comparison to the average impoverished income. The means to poach are readily available as arms imports to African countries have escalated. It is alleged that the strands of poaching networks reach into every strata of government and business life. The export routes tend to converge on those countries with the best communication and transport facilities, but every country adjoining the Zambezi has been implicated.

The odds of a poacher being apprehended are not high. Even if unlimited resources were available, the Zambezi would still prove difficult to patrol efficiently as it is too rugged and suffers from the further complication of encompassing international borders. The 'shoot on sight' policy implemented towards poachers is often justified on the basis that these insurgents use sophisticated weaponry. However, the policy is not an adequate deterrent, as there are simply too many people prepared to risk their lives. Consequently anti-poaching measures merely amount to no more than a holding action on the Zambezi.

We think the anti-poaching effort is failing. The governments concerned do not have, or are reluctant to commit, the necessary means to make it succeed. The World Wide Fund for Nature (WWF) withdrew their helicopter funding when Zimbabwe failed to demonstrate an effective rhino conservation policy. One of the reasons for failure is thought to be the dispersal of resources over too wide an area. If the entire effort was concentrated on one pocket of rhinos, perhaps their safety could be guaranteed.

At best, the black rhino is probably doomed to become a zoo animal. Efforts to halt demand for horn have failed dismally. CITES (Convention of Interna-

Kariba and Cahora Bassa have reduced the Zambezi's silt load, altering the balance of shoreline deposition and erosion. Mangroves are consequently dying along the seaward side of the delta.

tional Trade in Endangered Species) has, ever since its inception in the mid-1970s, banned trade in rhino products. The poaching dilemma needs to be tackled locally, nationally and internationally. Surely it is possible for concerned nations to coerce Taiwan, Zambia and others into global conservation of these vulnerable creatures? The plight of the rhino now depends largely on grassroots activists the world over.

### Dams: a route to the sea?

It is theoretically possible – if an additional seven dams are built on the Zambezi – for barges to ply between Victoria Falls and the sea. What is more, water could be diverted from the Zambezi at Kazangula and pumped over 1 000 kilometres to South Africa's industrial heartland on the Witwatersrand. On the way it would provide Botswana with irrigation. One can only commend man for his ingenuity, but at what cost? Perhaps it is appropriate to consider the following indictment against Cahora Bassa Dam.

'It is clear that in the case of Cahora Bassa there was no serious attempt to ecologically optimize the dam design prior to construction ... Furthermore, after dam closure, proposals put forward by the ecological impact assessment team were not implemented and there has been no regular monitoring of the dam's downstream effects during its seven-year lifespan ... As a result, Cahora Bassa has the dubious distinction from an ecological perspective of being the least studied and possibly the least environmentally acceptable major dam project in Africa. It is not clear why so little emphasis was placed on ecological considerations during the planning and post-planning phases of the dam project, but the 'hidden' long-term costs of this regrettable omission may be high if no attempts are made in the near future to assess the dam's detrimental effects and implement some forms of remedial action.' (Bernacsek, G.M. and Lopez, S., 1984).

We are stuck with Cahora Bassa. What guarantee have we that other projects will fare better? (Mupata and Batoka Dams are discussed in A Snare for Nyaminyami.)

## Pollution

The Upper Zambezi is the most unpolluted area I have ever visited. Caprivi was rather littered with refuse. Industrial pollution of the Zambezi is very low, the main problem being pesticides.

Since 1969 DDT has been the insecticide used on the largest scale in the fight against tsetse flies and mosquitoes in Zimbabwe, Zambia and Botswana. We have no hard data from Mozambique. W.R. Thomson (1984) expressed the view that 'the evidence supporting the contention that Zimbabwe has one of the most DDT-contaminated environments in the world is very great indeed'. J. Tannock *et al* (1983) reported levels of chlorinated hydrocarbons in Zimbabwean bird eggs. 'Material from Kariba showed considerable residue levels', he wrote, and suggested 'the population of raptors should be monitored carefully for indications of reproductive failure which might be attributable to pesticide residues'. A.T. Mhanga *et al* (1986) found that kapenta in the Ume tributary of Kariba Dam contained levels of DDT which were not a risk to human health. S. Mpofu (1987), even goes as far as to make a strong plea for the continued use of DDT.

Unfortunately, a DDT metabolite (DDE) causes thinning of bird eggshells by interfering with the action of the carbonic anhydrase enzyme within the shell-gland membrane. Adverse effects on reproduction can be so great as to lead to population extinction. Raptors are particularly vulnerable as they are at the top of the food chain and therefore accumulate the pesticide. Douthwaite and others have conducted a major survey of African Fish Eagles of the Zambezi. The results are not yet published but apparently indicate that the situation has deteriorated since earlier surveys and that the levels attained suggest the species is at risk. DDT is banned in most of the developed world, but is still preferred in Africa because it is cheap and effective, resistance is unusual and it is relatively non-toxic to humans.

*Cahora Bassa Dam: engineering triumph, political dilemma and ecological disaster.*

## Exotics

The aquatic macrophytes *Eichhornia crassipes* and *Salvinia molesta* are notorious examples of exotics that become troublesome. We saw plenty of *Lantana camara* near Victoria Falls. *Mimosa pigra* is a pest in Australia, but along the Zambezi seems to be contained to the banks by browsers. *Calotropis procera* is common on Cahora Bassa.

## Elephants

Since 1965 the rates of tree loss in Zimbabwe due to elephant damage have been unsustainable and from that time 44 500 elephants have been killed to try and reverse the trend. Presently the elephant population is about 52 000 with a natural increase of four to five per cent per annum. The evidence supporting Zimbabwe's elephant management policy is well outlined in a 1989 National Parks publication (see References). It is worth noting that the assumption was made 'that elephant will be adequately protected from illegal hunting'. Our suspicion is that this may not continue to be the case.

In October 1989 CITES voted to list the African elephant on Appendix 1, which means it is threatened with extinction and that there should be no further commercial trade in elephant products. The cataclysmic fall in elephant numbers in Africa is well known. There were over 1 000 000 in 1981 but only 622 000 in 1989. The chief reason for the decline is poaching for ivory.

Several African countries indicated that they would not honour the ivory trade ban. Instead a southern

African ivory trade cartel was proposed. The nations involved included Zimbabwe, Botswana, Malawi, Mozambique and Burundi. Zimbabwe and Botswana together have stable populations of over 100 000 elephants. Malawi has about 3 000 elephants, Mozambique's number is a guess and Burundi has none at all (but nevertheless exports considerable quantities of ivory). Burundi's motives were clearly not motivated by conservation; however, for the other 'rebels' the situation was different.

Proponents of the CITES ban believe that if ivory can be made worthless, no-one will shoot elephants for their tusks. They hope, by nullifying the market, to achieve this objective. Opponents point out that CITES bans have never wholly worked (as for example, with the black rhino). They feel poaching will only cease when a live elephant is worth more to the indigenous population (who have to live with elephants) than an illegal pair of tusks. They argue that the proceeds from elephant products can be spent on protecting the elephants and also to help the poor rural communities who suffer most from the ravages of elephants. (About 15 per cent of Zimbabwe's elephants live outside National Parks estate.) From 1981 to 1989 Zimbabwe obtained US$13 242 000 from elephant products. Elephants had a unit value of Z$12 400 in 1989 and provided 75 per cent of the total production of Nyaminyami District (a CAMPFIRE scheme).

Obviously the standard of elephant protection is not uniform across Africa and it may be that solutions to the poaching problem can differ and yet be equally successful. It is sad that the disputing parties, both championing the elephant cause, were unable to come to some sort of compromise. Meanwhile, in 1991, the elephant carnage continues.

## CONCLUSIONS

The preservation of Zambezi's genetic diversity involves two key concepts: active cooperation by its residents and full cognizance that manipulation of the river has both upstream and downstream consequences.

One of our motives for travelling the Zambezi was a fear that radical change was imminent and the river's present glorious nature may be irretrievably lost. Well, what do we think now? We see a glimmer of hope; nevertheless, time is desperately short for the magnitude of the task at hand and the odds cannot be good. We think the Zambezi will change as much in the next 50 years as it has during the last 150. If you can, visit the river now.

173

# REFERENCES AND FURTHER READING

Anonymous. 1989. 'Rhino poaching and anti-poaching strategy.' *The Zimbabwe Science News*. Vol. 23(7/8): 75.

Anonymous. 1989. *Policy for Wildlife*. Resources and Tourism, Dept. of National Parks and Wildlife Management, Zimbabwe.

Arnot, F.S. 1914. *Missionary travels in Central Africa*. John Wright & Sons Ltd., Bristol.

Baldwin, W.C. 1863. *African hunting and adventure from Natal to the Zambezi*. Richard Bentley & Son, London.

Bangs, R. 1985. 'Zambezi, a modern expedition.' In Bangs, R. and Kallen, C. *Rivergods: exploring the world's great wild rivers*. Sierra Club Books, San Francisco. pp. 25-41.

Bernacsek, G.M. and Lopez, S. 1984. 'Cahora Bassa.' In Kapetsky, J.M. and Petr, T. *Status of African reservoir fisheries*. Technical Paper No. 10. FAO, Rome.

Bond, W.J. 1975. 'The geology and formation of the Victoria Falls.' In: *Mosi oa Tunya: A handbook to the Victoria Falls region*. Longmans, London. pp. 19-27.

Bond, W.J. and Roberts, M.G. 1978. 'The colonization of Cahora Bassa, Mozambique, a new man-made lake, by floating aquatic macrophytes.' *Hydrobiologia*. Vol. 60: 243-259.

Bowler, M.C. 1988. 'Development Plans for the Lower Zambezi Valley.' *The Zimbabwe Science News*. Vol. 22(1/2): 3-4.

Brelsford, W.V. 1965. *Generation of men*. Stuart Manning Ltd., Salisbury, Rhodesia.

Brelsford, W.V. 1965. *The tribes of Zambia*. Government Printer, Lusaka, Zambia.

Chavunduka, G.L. 1981. 'Woodfuel: the present and future threat to rural and urban societies.' *The Zimbabwe Science News*. Vol. 15(1): 3-5.

Coppinger, M.P., Williams, G.D. and Maclean, G.L. 1988. 'Distribution and breeding biology of the African Skimmer on the Upper and Middle Zambezi River.' *Ostrich*. 59(3): 85-96.

Cumming, D. 1987. 'Zimbabwe and the conservation of Black Rhino.' *The Zimbabwe Science News*. Vol. 21(4/5): 59-61.

Curson of Kedleson, Lord. 1923. *Tales of travel*. London.

De Laessoe, H. 1908. 'The Zambezi River (Victoria Falls – Chinde). A boat journey of exploration, 1903.' *Rhodesia Scientific Association*. Vol. 13: 19-50.

Decle, L. 1898. *Three years in savage Africa*. London.

Du Toit, R.F. 1982. *A preliminary assessment of the environmental implications of the proposed Mupata and Batoka hydro-electric schemes (Zambezi River, Zimbabwe)*. NRB, Zimbabwe.

Du Toit, R.F. 1983. 'Hydrological changes in the Middle Zambezi system.' *The Zimbabwe Science News*. Vol. 17(7/8): 121-126.

Du Toit, R.F. 1987. 'Conservation biology of Black Rhino.' *The Zimbabwe Science News*. Vol. 21(4/5): 63-67.

Dunham, K.M. 1986. 'Movements of elephant cows in the unflooded Middle Zambezi Valley, Zimbabwe.' *African Journal of Ecology*. Vol. 24: 287-291.

Dunham, K.M. 1988. 'Demographic changes in the Zambezi Valley elephants (*Loxodonta africana*).' *Journal of Zoology, London. Vol. 215: 382-388.*

Dunham, K.M. 1989. 'Litterfall, nutrient-fall and production in an *Acacia albida* woodland in Zimbabwe.' *Journal of Tropical Ecology*. Vol. 5: 227-238.

Dunham, K.M. 1989. 'Long-term changes in Zambezi riparian woodlands, as revealed by photopanoramas.' *African Journal of Ecology*. Vol. 27: 263-275.

Environmental Consultants (Pvt) Ltd. 1990. *People, wildlife and natural resources – the Campfire approach to rural development in Zimbabwe*. The Zimbabwe Trust, Harare.

Fisher, W.S. and Hoyte, J. 1987. *Ndotolu – The life stories of Walter and Anna Fisher of Central Africa*. Lunda-Ndembu Publications, Zambia.

Gibbons, Major A. St. H. 1904. *Africa from North to South through Marotseland*. John Lane, London.

Gliwicz, Z.M. 1984. 'Limnological study of Cahora Bassa reservoir with special regard to sardine fishery expansion.' *FAO Project Field Document*. No. 6, Rome.

Guy, P.R. 1977. 'Notes on the vegetation types of the Zambezi Valley, Rhodesia, between the Kariba and Mpata Gorges.' *Kirkia*. Vol. 10(2): 543-557.

Handlos, W.L. and Howard, G.W. 1985. *Development prospects for the Zambezi Valley in Zambia*. Kafue Basin Research Committee, University of Zambia.

Holub, E. 1881. *Seven years in South Africa*. London.

Huckabay, J.D. 1987. *The Rocks in God's Highway*. Occasional study No. 14. Zambia Geographical Association.

Kenmuir, D.H.S. 1975. 'Sardines in Cahora Bassa Lake?' *New Scientist*. Vol. 13: 375.

Kenmuir, D.H.S. 1978. *A wilderness called Kariba*. Wilderness Publications, Salisbury.

Kerr, M.A. 1978. 'Reproduction of elephant in the Mana Pools National Park, Rhodesia.' *Arnoldia Rhod*. Vol. 29(8): 1-11.

Lamplugh, G.W. 1908. 'The gorges and basin of the Zambezi below the Victoria Falls, Rhodesia.' *Geog. Journ.* Vol. 31: 133-152.

Livingstone, D. and Livingstone, C. 1865. *Narrative of an expedition to the Zambezi and its tributaries*. John Murray, London. 608 pp.

Marshall, B.E. 1988. 'Why are the sardines so small?' *The Zimbabwe Science News*. Vol. 22(3/4): 31-35.

Martin, R.B., Craig, G.C. and Booth, V.R. 1989. *Elephant management in Zimbabwe*. Dept. of National Parks and Wildlife Management, Zimbabwe.

Mhanga, A.T., Taylor, R.D. and Phelps, R.J. 1986. 'HCH and DDT residues in the freshwater sardine at the Ume river mouth, Kariba.' *The Zimbabwe Science News*. Vol. 20(3/4): 46-48.

Mitchell, R.L. 1981. 'The Zambezi River: can Zimbabwe have a port? II: Technological and economic aspects.' *The Zimbabwe Science News*. Vol. 15(5): 123-126.

Mohr, E. 1876. *To the Victoria Falls of the Zambezi*. London.

Mpofu, S.M. 1987. 'DDT and its use in Zimbabwe.' *The Zimbabwe Science News*. Vol. 21(2/3): 31-36.

Murindagomo, R. 1989. 'The administration and management of wildlife in the communal lands: the case of Dande.' *The Zimbabwe Science News*. Vol. 23(7/9): 71-74.

Newton, I. 1984. 'Effect of organochloride pesticides on birds.' *Proc. 2nd Symp. African predatory birds*. Natal Bird Club, Durban.

Nugent, C. 1983. 'Channel changes in the behaviour of the Zambezi river at Nyambuomba.' *The Zimbabwe Science News*. Vol. 20(9/10): 121-131.

Nugent, C. 1987. 'Can the Zambezi irrigate the Kalahari?' *The Zimbabwe Science News*. Vol. 21(5/6): 68-70.

Nugent, C. 1988. 'The Zambezi river at Mana.' *The Zimbabwe Science News*. Vol. 22(1/2): 14-18.

Pangeti, G.N. 1988. 'The way ahead for indigenous resources in Zimbabwe.' *The Zimbabwe Science News*. Vol. 22(1/2): 19-20.

Phillipson, D.W. 1975. *Mosi-oa-Tunya. A handbook to the Victoria Falls region*. Longman, Rhodesia.

Pitman, D. 1989. *Elephants and people*. The Zimbabwe Trust, Harare.

Sangambo, M.K. 1979. *The history of the Luvale people and their chieftainship*. Ed. by R.J. Papstein. Mize Palace, Zambezi, Zambia.

Selous, F.C. 1881. *A hunter's wanderings in Africa*. Richard Bentley & Son, London.

Stanning, M.J. 1982. *Report on the economic impact to Zimbabwe of hydro-electric power development at Mupata and Batoka Gorges, from an environmental viewpoint*. NRB, Zimbabwe.

Swanepoel, C. 1988. 'The wildlife of the Mana Pools region.' *The Zimbabwe Science News*. Vol. 22(1/2): 24-28.

Tannock, J., Howells, W.W. and Phelps, R.J. 1983. 'Chlorinated hydrocarbon pesticide residues in eggs of some birds in Zimbabwe.' *Envir. Pollut.* (Series B), Vol. 5: 147-155.

Tatham, G.H. 1988. 'The rhino conservation strategy in the Zambezi Valley, code named Operation Stronghold.' *The Zimbabwe Science News*. Vol. 22(1/2): 21-23.

Taylor, R.D. 1982. 'Buffer zones, resolving the conflict between human and wildlife interests in the Sebungwe region.' *Zimbabwe Agricultural Journal*. Vol. 79(5): 179-183.

Taylor, R.D. 1987. 'Abundance and distribution of elephants in Matusadona National Park, Zimbabwe.' *Transactions of the Zimbabwe Scientific Association*. Vol. 63(6): 58-66.

Taylor, R.D. 1988. 'The indigenous resources of the Zambezi Valley: an overview.' *Zimbabwe Science News*. Vol. 22(1/2): 5-8.

Taylor, R.D. 1990. *Ecologist's report for 1989, Nyaminyami Wildlife Management Trust*. WWF Project No. 3749: Project paper No. 9, Harare.

Tello, J.L. 1986. *Wildlife cropping in the Zambezi delta, Mozambique*. Working party on Wildlife Management and National Parks, FAO, Rome.

Thomson, W.R. 1984. 'DDT in Zimbabwe.' *Proc. 2nd Symp. African predatory birds*. Natal Bird Club, Durban. pp. 169-171.

Tinley, K.L. 1969. 'First air count of the buffalo of Marromeu.' *Veterin. Mocamb.* Vol. 1(2): 155-170.

Tinley, K.L. 1971. 'Determinants of coastal conservation: Dynamics and diversity of the environment as exemplified by the Mozambique coast.' *Proc. of 'Nature conservation as a form of land use', Parque Nacional da Gorongosa SARCCUS symp.* pp. 125-153.

Tinley, K.L. 1973. 'Wildlife reconnaissance of the Mid-Zambezi valley in Mozambique before the formation of the Cahora Bassa dam.' *Veterin. Mozamb.* Vol. 6(2): 103-131.

Tinley, K.L. 1977. *Framework of the Gorongosa ecosystem*. DSc Thesis, Faculty of Science, University of Pretoria.

Trethowan, S.C. 1981. 'The Zambezi River: can Zimbabwe have a port? 1: Technical feasibility.' *The Zimbabwe Science News*. Vol. 15(5): 120-122.

Van der Vegte, J.H., Forster, C.W. and Forse, W.B. 1983. *Eastern Caprivi regional development strategy*. Environmental planning division of the N.P.A., Natal, South Africa.

Ward, P.R.B. 1979. 'Seiches, tides and wind set-up on Lake Kariba.' *Limnol. Oceanogr.* Vol. 24(1): 151-157.

Whitwell, A.C., Phelps, R.J. and Maclean, G.L. 1974. 'Further records of chlorinated hydrocarbon pesticides in Rhodesia.' *Arnoldia Rhod.* Vol. 6(37): 1-8.

Williams, G.D., Coppinger, M.P. and Maclean, G.L. 1989. 'Distribution and breeding of the Rock Pratincole on the Upper and Middle Zambezi river.' *Ostrich*. Vol. 60(2): 54-64.

Williams, F.L. 1974. 'African giant, the saga of the Cahora Bassa.' *Optima*. Vol. 24(3): 94-105.

# INDEX